Heal to Lead Wellness

Stories to Rebuild Your Confidence and Resilience

Volume Two

Raven + Grace
PRESS

RAVEN + GRACE PRESS

Contents

A Gift From the Authors

Throughout this book, we've shared powerful tools and practices that have guided us on our healing journeys, empowering us to lead with strength and purpose. Now, we want to extend these resources to you.

We've created a free collaborative digital workbook filled with valuable tools that accompany this book. Inside the digital workbook, you'll find prompts, strategies, mindset tools, meditations, and activities to start personalizing your own Heal to Lead journey.

To download, visit https://ravenandgrace.com/healtoleadwe2/.

It's our hope that these resources will enrich your experience and support you on your path.

With heartfelt gratitude,
The Authors of Heal to Lead Wellness

Introduction

At fifty years old, I was preparing to welcome my first grandson into the world. One day, my doctor said something that would stop my life in its tracks: I might not live long enough to see him grow up.

Those words echoed louder than anything I had ever heard. At that moment, time seemed to stand still. I imagined a little boy learning to walk, riding his bike for the first time, graduating high school, and becoming the man he was meant to be. Then I realized there was a real possibility I might not be there for any of it.

For most of my life, I carried the weight of more than just extra pounds. I had been the heaviest girl in my high school, and over time, that label became part of my identity. I learned how to quietly live behind that weight like a shield. I stayed silent so I wouldn't draw attention to myself. I avoided situations where I might feel exposed or uncomfortable. I mastered the art of hiding.

And hiding comes with a cost.

Without realizing it, I had missed so much of what makes life beautiful, friendships, adventures, laughter, and the simple joy of being fully present in the world.

Like so many people, I tried every new trend that promised quick results. Friends shared advice and miracle solutions, but nothing changed the deeper patterns that had shaped my life for decades.

Eventually, with a lot of dedication and work, I discovered that real change comes from small, consistent action. Step by step, habit by habit, things began to change. Slowly, the life that once felt impossible began to unfold.

Today, twenty-two years later, I no longer hide from life. I step into it. Now I stand at the top of mountains and look at the beauty below, realizing just how far I have come. As for that precious little boy I was so afraid I might never watch grow up, he is now twenty-two years old and weeks away from becoming a pilot.

And to think, I almost missed it.

That is why being part of *Heal to Lead Wellness* feels so meaningful to me.

The women in this book share powerful stories about facing life's challenges and choosing healing, resilience, and courage. Their journeys remind us that transformation rarely happens overnight, and that true change often begins with one small step, just as it did for me. Together, these stories show that our struggles do not define our limits. In many ways, they become the foundation for our strength and leadership.

My hope is that as you read, you find pieces of your own story within these chapters and the strength to take the next step toward your healing journey. May you have the courage, patience, and the belief that it is never too late to reclaim your life.

Cherryl Thompson
Author, *The Winding Road: Navigating the Path Back to You*

DÉJADA

(Abandoned)

Esmé Nemec

It was the kind of winter that couldn't quite make up its mind. The sun was shining like it had RSVP'd to a beach party, but the thermometer had other plans. Dr. George on ABC Channel 7 announced a high of forty-six degrees. Practically arctic for Southern California. Not as frigid as Queens, not as warm as New Orleans, just that peculiar in-between, the kind of cold that nips at you just enough to remind you you're alive.

And that day, I was.

Because Papi wasn't there.

Papi was tall, handsome, chestnut-skinned, with an accent that made women lean in a little closer—sometimes so close they practically risked falling into his shirt pocket. Momma had never met anyone like him. He came from Colombia, a country tied up in twenty-five years of knots and machismo, and then there was his story, the kind so dramatic it briefly made Momma's own hard-earned struggles look modest by comparison. A real-life epic: fleeing Colombia through the Darién jungle of raging rivers, pit vipers eager for a midday snack, humidity that could suffocate a saint, and malaria waiting like an impatient maître d'. He was trying to reach Europe to join his brother and study philosophy, only to be arrested in Costa Rica without a visa and rerouted to New York with the help of an attorney from his barrio in Bogotá.

Momma saw charm. She heard confidence. What she wanted was the kind of strength that made her feel safe. In truth, she was shrouded in a dense fog, wearily lifting, revealing a red, glowing exit sign she couldn't reach because the smoke was already in her lungs.

Gradually, the man who had once seemed loving began to vanish. His version of love came with bruises. A fist here, a foot there, nothing subtle about it. You learn quickly, in a house like that, that silence isn't just golden. It's armor.

Then came the day. Papi and Abuela were out, and Momma got her bold on. Fueled by equal parts fear and hope, she packed a suitcase, scooped up my hand, and off we went.

He quickly figured out where we had gone. Men like him have a sixth sense for when control begins to slip.

He promised to change, but of course, he didn't. The man who followed us south was the same one we'd left behind, same thunderclap temper, same mercurial moods, same fists.

Momma ran again, this time across the Mississippi, from the East Bank to the West Bank. My baby sister remained with Abuela. One evening, my regular babysitter was ill, Claire—a bona fide Cajun woman with the cooking skills of a trained chef. I loved Claire because she would scoop me up and wrap me in her arms, my head snuggled into her voluminous, pillowy assets. With no other options, Momma left me in the care of a "friend"—a hairy Turkish man she believed she could trust.

While Momma was serving wealthy lawyers and lovers dinner at the Maison Dupuy, the Turk was doing things no man should ever do to a child.

I never spoke of it. Not until my thirties wandered in like an uninvited supper guest, charming enough to forgive, reckless enough not to, poured themselves a tall, scandalously sweet Southern tea, leaded of course, and with a knowing smile, began thumbing through memories I'd very carefully kept under lock and key.

Papi found us again. So, Momma ran a third time. She scraped together what little she had, and we headed west with nothing but hope riding shotgun—New Orleans to Upland, California, an entire country between him and us.

Once Upon a Christmas Eve

It was Christmas Eve, just Momma, my toddler sister, me, and a man named Frank. Frank was kind, handsome, and Italian. He had a King Doberman named Dobie, a dog so big he had his own zip code. When Dobie slept beside me, I disappeared into the bed, small as a whisper. His heartbeat against mine was steady—boom, boom—like it was saying, "You're safe, I've gotcha."

That afternoon, Momma announced we had an errand to run. Through a language barrier and theatrical arm-flailing, she conveyed "put on your coat and gloves." We drove under rows of palm trees until I saw a sign:

WELCOME TO RANCHO CUCAMONGA

Now there's a name that can't decide whether it wants to be taken seriously or show up for comic relief.

We pulled into a mostly empty parking lot. Through the glass doors, a thick air of Christmas greeted us, cinnamon, pine, and something that felt a little holy. I stood in awe of the pyramid atrium. A grand Christmas tree rose through the center, with decorations that would make an angel feel underdressed.

A kind but very tired-looking woman came to the waiting area. She and Momma spoke in hushed tones; then Momma followed her through a door.

I sat in a lobby chair, swinging my legs, and waited.

When's Momma coming back? Circled my thoughts as I waited.

The woman returned. Smelling of honeysuckle, a hand resting gently on my shoulder, we walked down a long hallway in silence. Closed office doors lined the walls like quiet witnesses, the only light coming from beneath a door at the very end.

Surely Momma would be behind that door.

The honeysuckle lady pushed it open gently, and the fluorescent light hit my eyes.

Momma wasn't there.

Another woman entered, with big eyes framed by blue eyeshadow, thick mascara, a scarf perfectly knotted at her neck. *How sophisticated*, I thought, as if elegance could somehow make sense of the moment. She knelt in front of me as though handling something breakable, took my small hands in hers, and spoke gently.

"Te quedarás con una señora amable durante unos días, hasta que se pueda encontrar una familia con la que puedas vivir."

(You will stay with a lovely lady for a few days, until we arrange a family for you to live with.)

And that's when it landed.

Momma wasn't coming back. And where was my sister?

I rode in the scarf lady's car, silent and dazed. Whatever she said was just waa-waa-wonk, pure Charlie Brown adult speak. The sun had set, and the city streaked past the window in blurs of light I didn't bother to name. We pulled up to a small house with metal awnings striped in gray and white. A round woman with silver hair opened the door—kindness dressed up for Christmas, soft voice, warm eyes, an apron smelling of sugar and cinnamon.

She looked like Mrs. Claus.

I sat on her sofa while Mrs. Claus and the scarf lady spoke softly in Spanish.

"Pobrecita, y en Nochebuena. Me aseguraré de que tenga algo bajo el árbol por la mañana."

(Poor little thing, and on Christmas Eve. I'll make sure she has something under the tree in the morning.)

I remember thinking, *Would Momma be under the tree?* I knew it was ridiculous. How would she fit? But hope is wonderfully stubborn.

The next morning, Mrs. Claus made breakfast, calentado bogotano y cacao santafereño, topped with an overflowing pile of Christmas-colored mini marshmallows. A gloriously simple Colombian Sunday breakfast: seasoned fried rice with red beans, topped by a seasoned over-easy egg, and hot chocolate on the side. I slowly cut into the egg, gooey yolk spilling over the rice and beans.

I will never know how she knew that was my favorite meal. Maybe angels send memos.

After breakfast, she led me to the tree, knelt beside me, and whispered, "Creo que Papá Noel te encontró."

(I think Father Christmas found you.)

There was one gift, neatly wrapped with a shiny bow. Inside, una muñeca (a doll) with shoulder-length curls, a velvet dress, lace bobby socks, and glossy patent leather shoes. I named her Quita, short for muñequita (little doll), and from that moment on, she was my steadfast companion.

A few days later, the pretty scarf lady returned. Like a bookmark slipping between chapters, she moved me along. My next stop was a family with three kids, a little older than me.

Sadly, kindness wasn't part of their vocabulary.

My foster siblings didn't call me by my name. They called me Pobrecita (poor little thing) laced with sharp edges and giggles hiding behind too-small hands. Every day brought a barrage of nastiness.

"¿De qué basurero saliste?" they would spew.

(Which trash can did you crawl out of?)

They teased me for how little I had, for my dreadful bowl haircut, for not being with my "real" family, as if I'd filled out a request form for this life. After school, they played tag on the front lawn. My after-school activity was a sink of dishes stacked taller than my hope for a better day. After dinner, they disappeared to watch TV while I was sent to bed at seven o'clock sharp, daylight still pouring through the window like it was trying to keep me company.

Some houses have rules. And some houses have rulers.

The scarf lady visited every three weeks, always unannounced. On her third visit, the real kids were outside riding bikes, laughing, and being free. Me? Perched on a step stool, elbows deep in a sink of sudsy water. This time, something clicked.

Her eyes narrowed. She didn't say anything, but I could see her suspicions bloom. I wasn't being cared for. I was a free laborer with a state-funded check.

When her visit ended, she spoke with the foster parents in the next room. The husband's voice rose first, sharp, defensive, then volcanic. It confirmed everything she already knew.

She returned to the kitchen, voice soft, steady, purposeful. "Recoge tus cosas."

(Go ahead and gather your things.)

It didn't take long. Everything I owned, including Quita, fit into a woven plastic bag bright as confetti sprinkles. She took my hand, and just like that, another chapter closed.

Two months plus a week had passed.

Love and Fear Intertwined

The next house was a two-story townhouse with a staircase that felt like something out of a fairy tale. If houses could flirt, this one was giving it a go. The couple was young, childless, and seemed gentle. But by then, hope was something I handled with oven mitts, always waiting for the burn.

Momma started visiting after a few months. Every other weekend or so, she showed up, and each time my heart did a strange little dance, wanting to run into her arms and hide behind the couch at the same time. She would smell the same, hold me the same, and then leave the same. Love and fear had become Siamese twins inside me.

For nearly a year, that became the rhythm, little reunions followed by long stretches of waiting. Then one day, she didn't take me back. We disappeared.

Once back in Louisiana, she brought me to an apartment in the New Orleans suburb of Metairie. The air in New Orleans clung to your skin like a damp, dirty blanket. Everything felt louder and heavier—the horns, the arguments drifting through thin walls. Even the silence had an edge.

And then Momma left again.

The apartment was musty, dark, and dismal. Roaches marched across the counters like they paid rent. Their baby was habitually left in an overflowing nappy. The husband was a greasy New Orleans police officer; the wife was grotesquely large and smelled. She didn't yell or huff. She just whipped.

Many months later, I missed the school bus. I couldn't bear another one-on-one conversation with that belt. "A belt whipping a day to keep the naughty away" was her motto, and she is forever remembered as the smelly belt lady. That day, a teacher found me lingering on the playground and drove me to the pigsty. I sat stiffly the whole way, dread pooling in my stomach like something sour.

That evening, I lay bruised on a thin mattress on the floor, listening. The smelly belt lady's voice sliced through the walls. "Just come and get the little brat!"

Was she talking to Momma?

The next evening, Saturday, January 14, was dry and cold. A man, an attorney, arrived at the door in a polyester suit. As the smelly belt lady ranted beside him, he exhaled one of those deep, tired breaths a man masters only after years with a wife who could out-argue a thunderstorm.

He crouched to my level and said the familiar words. "Recoge tus cosas."

(Gather your things.)

As usual, it didn't take long. I climbed into the front seat of his car with Quita, enveloped by the smell of leather, a scent I would find comforting for the rest of my life. He buckled me in. My coat was zipped to my chin, my hands trembling in my pockets. Fear sat beside me; this was the first time I had been alone with a man since the Turk.

He said he was taking me somewhere better.

I didn't say a word. I just watched the streetlights slide across the dashboard, one by one. But somewhere inside me, in a place that hadn't felt warm in a long while, something flickered.

Hope on Training Wheels

Traffic was heavy on the I-10 that night, inchworm slow. Our silence was broken only by sharp car horns. I was exhausted, and my body ached. I succumbed to the sleep that knocked at my mental door.

He gently woke me as he pulled into the driveway of a big, clean, beautiful house with a winding path and small lights guiding the way to a grand front door. Silhouettes moved inside warm rooms. It was a picture-postcard kind of home.

That's where I met my new mom and dad.

I may have arrived sleepy, small, and quiet, but I came armed with the kind of attitude only a wounded child can muster. They had signed up for a daughter and got a hot little mess with trust issues.

My new dad was really tall, six-foot-six, exuding warmth and calm. Firm jaw-line, glasses, very curly hair that, I later discovered, was a perm common among men in the seventies. A music minister from Pensacola, Florida, with a voice straight out of heaven. He had sung in operas and recorded Christian albums. Kind and patient, even when I stepped out of line, his voice stayed steady and loving. When he hugged you, it felt like a promise.

My new mom was reserved, petite, and looked so small standing next to him. Long blonde curls, pretty clothes, intoxicating perfume, and the soft lilt of an East Texas drawl, a real lady with quiet strength. A schoolteacher, she believed in standards and structure and somehow understood my history. It didn't take her long to realize I didn't have a cavity-free tooth in my mouth, my handwriting was nonexistent, and my grasp of English was choppier than rusty scissors cutting wet paper. She was patient. Every word I learned with her became love and belonging.

It took time to earn my trust. I'd never known boundaries that didn't hurt, and I was wary of mistaking affection for love. But slowly, I learned the difference—a vast valley of distance— between the smelly belt lady's "affection" and my new parents' unending love. I finally had a home and people to call my own.

Fractured Pieces Becoming Whole

I often return, in my mind, to that Christmas-tree atrium, the smell of cinnamon and pine, the empty chair where my mother should have been.

And sometimes I think of Quita. Unbeknownst to me then, she was a little life raft whispering, "Stay. Don't disappear."

My childhood story doesn't end there, but my new family served as the foundation for everything that followed, proof that even the most fractured beginnings can grow into something steady and astonishing.

Life has a wicked sense of humor when it comes to green lights. They often arrive disguised as heartbreak. Mine appeared in waiting rooms and quiet car rides, in roaches pulling up a chair for dinner, and most importantly, in the arms of new parents who loved me long before I knew how to trust them.

For years, I mistook silence for strength, telling myself I could outrun the echo of every slammed door and every goodbye.

But healing comes in stillness.

When you sit with the ache long enough, what once felt like a threat becomes an invitation. The pain teaches you that the very thing that breaks you sets you free. As maturity settled in, I turned confusion, fear, and misplaced love into clarity, compassion, and purpose. Our psyche tucks away little trauma reminders, a warm ember, waiting for the right breeze. When that breeze finally stirs, the whole thing sparks to life. Some call this reliving the pain. I call it a tilt, the moment the experience shifts into perspective, fear redefines itself as focus, and loss starts doing its best impression of legacy. The clarity that follows is what reshapes us.

The road has been long and winding. I enlisted in the Army, went on to university, became an Air Force officer, and served a long and distinguished career. From Louisiana humidity to the deserts of Southwest Asia and a thousand landscapes in between, I have made mistakes and discovered that mistakes paired with meaning are simply tuition for becoming your future self.

When I meet people standing at their own crossroads, I tell them what I wish someone had said to that little girl on Christmas Eve.

You don't have to be unbreakable to be whole.

You must be willing to stay and own your past.

And the moment you can look at your story and say, "That was real, and it mattered."

You've stepped into your green light.

What Tried to Kill Me Called Me

A Story of Rebirth

Carrie Polk

I used to be known as the happy-go-lucky farm girl! You know the one with dirt under my nails, hair French-braided, overalls covering my girlish figure, smiling big enough to overshadow the worry of the day. Mom and I ran the farm like we were singing a rhythm we never had to practice. She planted wisdom and strength; I planted tomatoes and flowers.

People depended on us for their food needs in the community. We both ran the business like we were twining life together. Mom and I were inseparable, knowing each other's thoughts by just looking at one another. I was an anchor in the ground like Mom, who so many in our community depended on. Numerous families waited for us to deliver their CSA bags every week, and we were anchors at the regional farmer's market, restaurants counted on our weekly produce deliveries, and whenever someone needed food, flowers, or a little hope delivered with a smile, they called me. I swung sixty-pound hay bales without thinking, organized delivery routes before breakfast, and still had enough energy left to cook supper for our farm crew. I felt strong, steady, and rooted in the farmland I called home.

There is a confidence that I built as a farmgirl that comes from belonging to the soil and every season of the year. It is rooted in the thought that each year of life will always return the way Spring does, faithful, predictable, and stronger than the year before. I thought nothing could shake me other than my God. I believed my life was safe, strong, and unbreakable. I had no idea that everything I knew of myself was about to vanish.

You know how you see on the news those moments that split a life clean in two. But for some reason, you just don't correlate those events that could possibly be near. Those before, and after that, no one prepares you for. Mine didn't arrive loudly. It came through violence, the kind people whisper about because they don't know how to carry it. One moment, I was Carrie, a farmer, daughter, the familiar girl with sunburned cheeks and a rosy sunburnt nose. The next jolting moment, I was no longer sure I would live long enough to remember my very own name.

Hovering in the Unknown

With the last breath I could feel, I thought one thing—just instinct clawing for breath and life.

"Jesus." There was absolutely no eloquence or promise in my whisper, just a plea for life. And then everything went black. The memories from that moment until days later are hidden somewhere deep.

But the terror of those days that followed left their mark on me, smothered in fear, detached from humanity, and scared of all humanity, even my very own self. Life was different and unrecognizable now. I never learned or was ever told anything about this kind of life.

The air smelled wrong—sharp, metallic, suffocating. My heart slammed against my ribs like a panicked animal trying to escape from its prey. I tried to speak, but my voice didn't come out, trapped somewhere between my chest and the terror locking my throat. My body wouldn't obey me. It went limp, cold, and still as I realized I had been abducted.

And then something even more terrifying happened.

They raped and tortured me. As the days went on, it was as though my mind left, and I was suddenly watching myself from somewhere else. I was detached, floating as if my life were happening through a see-through door, and I was no longer inside it. I understood at that very moment that this is how people disappear forever. You know, like those stories on the news we've all seen. Terror and fright in your mind, they don't scream. They are silent, wretched, and merciless.

At some point, my eyes opened. I was alive, yes, but lifeless, and I knew I had to find the strength to escape.

I did.

Honestly, it's revolting to me how many people romanticize survival, because survival is messy. It strips your pride, dignity, and respect clean out of the way. I woke in a body I barely recognized, bruised inside and out, muscles forgotten, my words tangled when I went to speak, my thoughts and sentences misfired like baking soda mixed with vinegar, it spewed everywhere.

As the weeks went on, I tried to speak, and instead of "barber shop," I said "butcher shop." When people laughed softly, thinking it was sweet and funny, they didn't know it cut me to the core and hurt like daggers. I couldn't hear the wrong words that my brain misfired from Post Traumatic Stress Disorder (PTSD). I only felt the humiliation of no longer having my normal abilities working properly. I became angry at my brain that refused to obey me, and that didn't present me with dignity.

Every day, my mind felt slow, thick, and confused, as if I were wading through clay. Every sentence felt like climbing a mountain barefoot.

A Mother's Love

Through it all, my mother stayed by my side, believing in me with unconditional love. My doctors finally gave up on me, sending me home with no rehab, just for me to gracefully slip onto the other side. But that "twining" Mom of mine, she didn't leave my bedside, not for a night, not for a shift change in the hospital or at home in a hospital bed. She didn't doubt for a moment, even when hope looked foolish, or my temperature hit one-hundred-four. She knew her twin would be beside her again someday. She brushed my hair, tended to my wounds, rolled me, changed me, fed me, and washed me like when I was her baby, every single day. She slept right beside me like a mother with a newborn. Whether it was a chair or a sleeping bag on the hard floor, she was there. When the medical world pulled back, saying they didn't know what to do or they did all they could do, she leaned in closer with faith, strength, and belief that I would one day lead again. When others stepped away, Mom stepped toward me. Her love and unwavering faith held me to this earth when everything else let go. Hearing her daily cries and prayers to God gave me the strength to fight the battle to live.

Nearly a year passed before I managed my first shower. You don't understand sacredness until something so simple becomes impossible. I remember that day as if it were yesterday. Mom was wheeling me down her hallway in Grandma's wheelchair for my first shower.

The shower chair and shower bar looked like Mount Everest to my mind. My legs trembled, my breath shook as Mom asked if the temperature of the water was too warm, but Mom held me steady with her small frame, getting soaked in the shower water as well. Her hand on my back was my security and lifeline as I sat on that shower chair. The warm water ran over my skin, and I felt exposed, fragile, yet terrified I would fall and drown.

The whole ordeal of showering only lasted a few minutes, but when it was over, I collapsed back into the hospital bed in my room (which was Mom's family room), exhausted to the bone, crying from something deeper than pain. It was from the fierce miracle that I had done what I wasn't sure I ever could.

Healing was not measured in leaps and bounds, but in inches and beliefs in miracles. I began trying to rise from a wheelchair. I took my first step, holding on to Mom for dear life. I tried many times to shuffle and walk with my finger tips brushing Mom's walls for balance, and finally learned to walk again. Ten shaky steps soloing my walk across the family room with no wall or furniture to grab onto was terrifying, but with Mom cheering me on like a baby taking its first steps, it was scary, but I made it, falling into her arms.

Hiding the Pain

Eventually, Mom took me to the farm, but it wasn't the same. Why? Because I wasn't the same. Customers needed their produce, not a sick owner who said they would have to wait a while. They needed eggs and apples, and the list goes on.

I am not sure how, amongst the rehab Mom did for me, she managed to keep the farm business afloat. That part of her is a strength only God can give her. Someone at the farm had to take orders, deliver bags, smile, and make small talk. So, eventually, I put on a mask as a cheerful farm girl, the one I used to be.

I struggled to walk the uneven fields without shaking legs and falling. I packed produce, hoping no workhand or customer would notice my trembling hands and weak arms that could barely lift a single tomato into a bag. I laughed and smiled even though inside I was drowning in fear and pain that made me feel like dying.

Trauma is heavy, but silence is heavier on your mind and soul. When tragedy hits you, it's as though people grow uncomfortable around you. Some avoid you like you have a plague. Some gossip, and that stings to your core. Some pretend they don't see your scars in front of their face. Yet others forget you're human. I learned almost instantaneously to hide my pain, fragility, and fear, because brokenness made others uneasy.

Shame grew like invasive weeds inside me, crowding out self-love and allowing self-hatred to set in. Making myself worth falling to zero. Every car that pulled into the farm made fear shoot through me, and panic mode kicked in, giving me the urgency to run and hide. I mistrusted men to the point that I was scared of them and rarely even spoke to them. I hated the version of me that survived. I was weak and slow. The girl who could once lift bushels of cabbage now needed help just to walk across the gravel driveway. I didn't know who I was, or how to ever become whole again. The only thing I knew to do was to lean into my faith and believe it was true.

Sprouts From the Soil

Healing came ever so slowly and quietly, like spring beneath frozen ground when the daffodils spring forth. In the early mornings, Mom and I walked the pasture side by side, our boots pressing into damp earth as the sun rose slowly and forgiving. The farm became my nonjudgmental therapist. She was there for me, steady, unflinching, willing to hold what I couldn't. Offering me what she offered to nature.

A new season and another chance to blossom. I rebuilt my strength the only way I knew how, by working the land, because the medical community deemed me hopeless to live. I pulled weeds until my hands burned, and with every root I tore from the soil, something else came loose inside me—the anger at what had been done to me, the bitterness toward my body for betraying me, the self-hatred that whispered I would never be whole again. The ground didn't recoil from my fury. It received it.

In the greenhouse, I planted seeds with trembling hands, pressing them into the soil like prayers. I wasn't brave enough to speak aloud because I couldn't bear the sound of it. I wasn't just growing food anymore. I was now begging for something inside me to grow back. Love, grace, forgiveness, and a new me. I needed a reason to live again and have a purpose that was deeper than ever before. Some days, I cried hard enough that I felt as though I was watering five acres of vegetables, my tears soaking into the dirt. Other days, I sat in the barn staring at nothing, suspended between who I had been and who I didn't yet know how to become. I was just there, still numb and wondering what's next.

Then there were the days that anger roared inside of me so fiercely at what I had become. With fists clenched, I screamed into the wind, "Why? Why me? Why my body? Why my life?"

The words tore out of me because fear had nowhere else to go. It lived in my bones, in my breath, in the way my heart leapt at every sound. Shame told me I was weak for not moving on faster. Trauma told me I was no longer safe in my own skin. The farm bore witness to it all, my rage, my grief, my exhaustion.

Slowly, something shifted inside of me. Between the screams and the silence, between the questions and the tears, the anger began to loosen its grip. It didn't disappear, but it softened. Fear and anxiety still visited and had a firm grip on me, but they no longer ruled every breath. I noticed moments when my chest didn't feel so tight, and I could actually sleep without a nightmare. I had several days when I actually could inhale without bracing for impact. I could see the sprouts of life returning inside. They were fragile, brief, but undeniable, present within me.

Gentle Wings

One morning, sitting on the porch, a female cardinal landed on a branch sitting on the banister beside me. Still. Unafraid. Her presence felt so intentional, as if she was sent by the Creator to talk to me. It was a quiet yet welcoming interruption to my morning.

I didn't hear a voice, but something inside me knew. This is not the end. Rebirth is already happening in you.

I sat there staring at this cardinal longer than I meant to, watching her breathe, listening to her chirp. She literally landed on my shoulder and kept talking. Quietly, she flew away. Every morning for about a month, I would go out to sit on the porch and watch for her. She would come and talk, leaning on the banister and the chair for a while, and then fly away. The thoughts came to me that healing didn't arrive like a lightning strike. Healing came with a gentle touch. Unexpectedly. Real. Consistent and with beauty and dignity.

As I healed, women with deep wounds began showing up in ways I didn't expect. They called, texted, and messaged wanting produce or eggs, but they left pieces of their hearts in my hands. They had stories of their own of miscarriages, illness, divorce, and trauma. They'd stand with me beside crates of zucchini and suddenly share wounds they hadn't dared to speak to anyone else.

Deep pain recognizes deep pain, and spirits connect when they are heard. I soon realized the very parts of my story I wanted hidden forever were the very parts that made women feel safe, comfortable, and loved. It was amazing to me how something as simple as selling a dozen eggs to someone could give a woman the love they needed to make it through the day. That is when I realized what tried to kill me became the very ground my calling grew from.

I didn't need to be fully healed to lead. I only needed to take humanity, women by the hand, and rise alongside them. My farm has turned into a sanctuary. My story has become a lantern. My scars on my arms are visible scars for the world to see that once my self-hatred, fear, and humiliation that came from trauma and abuse finally became something beautiful. It became my authority to speak of hope, life, and self-love.

Somewhere in my spirit, the stillness of my faith, in the slow rebuilding of my strength and health, I found purpose, true love, and dignity to lead humanity back to wholeness. It was no longer the old purpose of pushing through and pleasing people with a mask of despair on the other side, but a deeper one, a true purpose that one carries with you. It became my sword, a shield, and a readiness to guide women out of the same darkness that swallowed me. It is what helps them heal in body, mind, and spirit, and reminds them they are more than what happened to them.

If you are reading this broken, afraid, unsure of who you are now, let your heart hear that you are not too far gone! The fact that you are still breathing means purpose is still alive in you. Trauma isn't the end of life; it may be the birthplace of your calling if you allow it.

You don't have to rise perfectly. You just try to rise, even if it's slow, even if you tremble, even if you crawl. You will learn to fly again, just like that female cardinal told me I could do as she chirped on my shoulder. You can heal and be put back together as a new creation, stronger than before. You can still lead yourself and even others. You can live again. You can love yourself again and know there is a flower budding inside you, ready to bloom. It won't be the same life as you once had, but a new life.

Remember, you are not what was done to you! Never forget that. You are who you become after. Your rebirth is awaiting you. There is a purpose being formed inside you during the darkness. And when you whisper, "God help", heaven listens.

The Comeback

FROM DIAGNOSIS TO PURPOSE

Elana Hilf

I never set out to start a nonprofit, especially not in the chronic illness space. But life has a way of steering you into unexpected chapters, and I quickly realized we could either be overwhelmed by what happened to us or transform it into something meaningful.

For our family, that moment came the day my oldest son, Gavin, was diagnosed with Type 1 diabetes (T1D). One minute we were living our normal, busy life—school, sports, carpools, homework, dinners on the fly, repeat. Next, we were sitting in a hospital hearing words that landed like a punch to the gut.

"Autoimmune disease. Lifelong. Incurable."

And just like that, life split into before and after.

If you've ever been handed news that instantly rewrites your future, you know the feeling. Your mind races ahead before your heart can catch up. You're thinking about tomorrow, next year, while trying to stay calm enough not to scare the person you love most. That was me. Standing there, nurses crowded around his hospital bed, watching Gavin learn how to prick his finger to check his blood sugar and give himself insulin injections, skills no child should have to master, while silently wondering how I was supposed to carry my own fear without letting it spill onto him.

Type 1 diabetes doesn't ease you in gently. It demands attention immediately. Every meal becomes math, counting carbohydrates. Every activity requires pre-planning. Do we have enough insulin with us and low blood sugar snacks to survive? Every night carries a low hum of *Is he okay, and waiting for his blood sugar alarm to go off and wake up the whole house at 2 a.m.* It's exhausting and emotional, and it's invisible to most people. What surprised me the most wasn't just the medical overwhelm, it was the loneliness.

The Quiet Isolation No One Warns You About

Even surrounded by incredible doctors, supportive friends, and loving family, there was a space that felt oddly empty. Gavin was suddenly the kid with a chronic disease. The one living with lifesaving medical devices on his body 24/7. The one who needed snacks to survive. The one whose parents hovered.

And I was suddenly *that mom*, the one who worries all the time. The one constantly checking, planning, mentally running through worst-case scenarios. My nervous system felt completely jacked up, always on high alert, as I could never fully relax again.

I remember those nights not long after diagnosis. The house would finally go quiet, and everyone else would fall asleep, but I couldn't. I would sit on the edge of Gavin's bed in the dark, my phone glowing as I stared at his blood sugar app; they were numbers I was still trying to understand.

I kept refreshing the screen, trying to figure out what might happen next. My body was exhausted, but my mind refused to shut off. I was terrified to fall asleep. What if his blood sugar dropped too low during the night? What if I didn't hear the alarm?

So I would sit there and force myself to stay awake, watching the numbers, watching him breathe, silently praying they would stay steady, ready to triage a blood sugar crisis at any moment. Unless you've lived inside the world of Type 1 diabetes, it's hard to explain the weight of those nights, the sleeplessness, constant listening for alarms, and the quiet fear that sits in the back of your mind, wondering, *Will my child wake up tomorrow?* Suddenly, the responsibility of keeping your child alive feels like it's resting entirely on your shoulders. The margin for error feels impossibly small, and the weight of that responsibility feels unbearable.

There is a part of your soul that quietly breaks when you live with that fear night after night, wondering if your child will wake up the next morning. Even surrounded by loving friends and family, those nights can feel incredibly isolating, because the weight of that responsibility is something only another Type 1 parent can truly understand.

At the time, I didn't realize it yet, but moments like that were quietly planting the seed for something I would one day feel called to create, because no family should ever have to carry that kind of weight alone.

Healing Started With Awareness

Before this chapter of my life, I had already reinvented myself more than once. I left a successful corporate marketing career of many years in 2016 to pursue more self-led, purpose-driven work. I became a children's yoga teacher, helping kids build confidence, emotional awareness, and resilience through movement and mindfulness. Later, during the pandemic, I pivoted again and built a real estate investment company, learning, yet again, that growth usually arrives disguised as disruption. When Type 1 diabetes entered our lives, something in me recognized the pattern. This wasn't just something to "get through." This was something to grow through, but first, I had to do the inner work.

I had to acknowledge the fear instead of pretending I was fine. The fear that my child's safety now depended on decisions I had to make every single day. The quiet, overwhelming weight of knowing that a wrong call, or a moment of hesitation, could have serious consequences.

Before Type 1 diabetes, I imagined motherhood filled with scraped knees, playdates, and homework at the kitchen table. I expected to guide my children through life's ordinary challenges, not carry the responsibility of helping keep my child alive through medical decisions. That original version of motherhood disappeared overnight.

To move forward, I had to grieve the life I thought we would have so I could fully step into the one we were given. I realized something important. I couldn't create a calm space for my child until I did the work to calm myself. When the overwhelm would rise, I turned to small practices throughout the day, pausing to meditate, listening to binaural beats, slowing my breathing, anything that could calm my nervous system and bring me back to center.

Healing, I learned again, is an active decision, one to rise with courage even when my heart feels heavy. A decision to keep showing up even when everything inside me feels uncertain. Because when your child looks to you for safety, courage becomes non-negotiable, and love becomes the strength that carries you forward, even when you don't know how you'll keep going.

The Question That Sparked Everything

One day, somewhere between counting carbs and sitting in my car after yet another doctor's appointment, a quiet question surfaced. *What if this isn't happening to us but for us?* Not in a toxic-positivity, "everything happens for a reason" kind of way, but in a grounded, honest, now what? kind of way.

I started looking for spaces where kids with Type 1 diabetes could simply be themselves locally and run, play, laugh, devices on full display, without having to stop mid-fun to explain why they wear an insulin pump (what we jokingly call their "robot pancreas").

Gavin had been lucky enough to attend a few T1D summer camps, and they were incredible. For the first time since his diagnosis, I saw him surrounded by kids who truly understood his life. He looked relaxed and confident again. However, those camps only happened once a year. I wanted something more consistent, something local where kids and families could connect throughout the year. When I began searching for it, I quickly realized there wasn't a community like that nearby.

That was when the thought shifted from *Someone should create this* to *maybe we're the ones meant to*. Then it hit me. I realized I could use the skills I'd gathered through different seasons of my life—the event planning and organizational experience from years as a marketing and promotions director, the children's programming skills from running my kids' yoga franchise, and the business instincts I'd developed from building my property group.

Those seemingly unrelated chapters suddenly felt connected, pointing toward the same purpose: creating a thoughtful, well-run nonprofit community for kids and families living with Type 1 diabetes. Instead of waiting for the perfect group to appear, we did what life sometimes asks of us, and we built it ourselves.

Enter: T1D Allstars

T1D Allstars was created from a mother's instinct, a need for a regulated nervous system, and a very clear belief that kids with Type 1 diabetes are not fragile. They are powerful, incredibly resilient, and they deserve environments that reflect that.

I hit the ground running, and we began hosting free, sports-based meetups across South Florida, at various athletic facilities, with a different sport focus each time, movement-driven events where kids could push their limits, learn something new, build confidence, and meet others just like them to connect. Just movement, connection, and community. Then something magical happened. Kids who walked in shy walked out laughing with new friends. Parents who arrived tense left lighter. Families stopped feeling alone. What I realized in real time was that healing accelerates when it's shared.

Community: The Missing Piece of Healing

There is something so deeply calming about being in a space where you don't have to explain yourself. Where people just understand your lived experience. When kids see other kids wearing medical devices and still running and playing like nothing is holding them back, something inside them softens and connects. When parents hear the words "me too," not as sympathy, but as knowing, it's like you can finally take a full breath again.

In those moments, Type 1 diabetes stops being the center of everything. It becomes part of the playbook, not the whole story. That's when the nervous system begins to settle. The constant tension eases. The feeling of being on high alert starts to melt, even just a little. Healing doesn't always come from fixing or solving. Sometimes it comes from simply being surrounded by people who make you feel safe, seen, and less alone. That's what T1D Allstars has become. More than an organization, it's a place where connection is the medicine. Where joy is still possible, and where families can move forward together, one moment of community at a time.

Looking back on those early days after diagnosis, life often felt heavy, like we were carrying something invisible that few people around us could understand. But now, when our family walks into a T1D Allstars event, the feeling in the room is completely different. Kids with insulin pumps and CGMs are cheering each other on like it's the most normal thing in the world. Their devices beep, and no one even notices. Seeing a cool new pump or patch sparks excitement, and instead of hiding their devices, kids wear them proudly as life-saving technology.

Parents share stories, advice, and offer the kind of understanding that doesn't require explanation. The fear and responsibility of this disease still exist, of course. But they no longer live in the same lonely silence. Now they are held inside a community, one where Gavin and every child living with Type 1 diabetes can see they are not the only ones walking this path, and where families are reminded that we were never meant to carry this alone.

What Is Type 1 Diabetes?

For anyone unfamiliar with Type 1 diabetes, it helps to understand what this diagnosis really means. It's not the kind of "diabetes" most people casually think of; it's usually not what "your grandma has" or what "your dog or cat has" (we hear that a lot).

More than two million people in the U.S. live with Type 1 diabetes, including over three-hundred-thousand children and teens, and diagnoses are rising about 3% each year. Thousands of families suddenly find themselves navigating this disease every year, which is exactly why connection, education, and community support matter. Type 1 diabetes is a lifelong autoimmune disease with no cure. It happens when the immune system mistakenly attacks the pancreas and stops it from producing insulin, a hormone the body needs to survive.

Insulin allows sugar from food to move out of the bloodstream and into the body's cells for energy. Without it, sugar builds up in the blood, and the body can quickly become very sick. That's why people with Type 1 diabetes have to depend on insulin to stay alive.

From the moment of diagnosis, a person suddenly has to do the job their pancreas once did automatically: taking insulin through injections or pumps and constantly monitoring blood sugar using continuous glucose monitors, the small devices you may notice on someone's arm sending readings to their phone every few minutes, day and night. Researchers estimate people with Type 1 diabetes make about one-hundred-eighty extra health-related decisions every day, constantly calculating and adjusting just to stay safe. That level of nonstop responsibility can lead to real mental and emotional burnout.

It's also important to know that Type 1 diabetes is not the same as Type 2 diabetes. Type 1 is autoimmune; the body stops making insulin. Type 2 means the body still produces insulin, but doesn't use it effectively. Type 1 has nothing to do with diet, sugar intake, or lifestyle choices, and it's not something a parent or child caused. It can appear at any age, often in families with no history of the disease at all.

Another common misunderstanding is people often think someone with Type 1 diabetes shouldn't eat sugar. Ironically, sugar can sometimes be lifesaving. When blood sugar drops too low, a person with T1D must eat sugar immediately to bring it back up. Living with Type 1 is a constant balancing act, sometimes taking insulin to bring blood sugar down, and sometimes eating sugar to bring it back up.

Because Type 1 diabetes can appear suddenly, recognizing the warning signs matters. Symptoms may include extreme thirst, frequent urination, sudden weight loss, exhaustion, blurry vision, fruity-smelling breath, or rapid breathing. When several appear together, a simple blood sugar test can help prevent a dangerous emergency called diabetic ketoacidosis (DKA). Catching Type 1 early can be lifesaving.

Today, Type 1 diabetes can sometimes even be detected early through a blood test that identifies T1D autoantibodies, sometimes before insulin is immediately needed. Early screening options are becoming more available through doctors and research programs. (FOOTNOTE)

https://www.breakthrought1d.org/early-detection/

The truth is, living with Type 1 diabetes can feel like having another full-time job, except sometimes the employee is a child. And yet, with today's technology and support, kids with T1D can live big, active lives. They can play sports, chase dreams, and thrive. One of the most powerful forms of support is community. That kind of connection is so important, and it's exactly why groups like T1D Allstars matter, until the day we hopefully find a cure.

How My Healing Journey Turned Into Leadership

I didn't create T1D Allstars because I had everything figured out. I created it because I was willing to walk forward anyway, through the unknown, through the ashes and dust of my old life. There's a famous saying, "The only way out is through," and it's really true. The only way out of a terrible experience is to walk through the fire and come out on the other side. Maybe you're burned and bruised, but you're not broken. There is still a full life waiting on the other side of heartbreak.

Through this journey, I learned that leadership doesn't require perfection; it requires presence and persistence. It requires being honest about where you've been and brave enough to say, "If this helped me, maybe it can help you too." My son's diagnosis changed our family, but it also clarified my purpose. It showed me that healing expands when we create space for others to heal alongside us.

There is no going back. There is only rising, stronger, wiser, more connected. Gavin isn't defined by T1D; he's defined by his courage, living life every day alongside a life-altering diagnosis. Today, Gavin is a thriving teenager. He's hanging out with friends, making his own plans, learning how to drive, and stepping into the independence every teenager craves. The difference is that he carries a responsibility most kids his age never have to think about: managing a serious disease and quite literally keeping himself alive. That responsibility may stay with him until a cure is found, but over time, the management becomes part of the rhythm of life. You adapt because living fully is the only choice.

Our family believes deeply that nothing will stop Gavin from following his dreams. We remain hopeful that a cure will be found in his lifetime. Until that day comes, we'll keep building T1D Allstars, connecting families, lightening the emotional burden of this disease through community, and raising awareness for a future without it.

What once felt like overwhelming darkness has slowly been replaced by determination, community, and purpose, and gratitude that something meaningful could grow from it. We are hopeful, and we know that when families come together, even the heaviest burdens become lighter to carry.

What I Hope You Take With You

If there's one thing I hope this story leaves you with, it's that your hardest chapter may be preparing you for your most meaningful work in this world. Sometimes, the thing that feels like it knocked you off course is actually the beginning of your greatest comeback, one filled with purpose, community, and a whole lot more connection and love than you ever expected.

When you choose inner healing, when you regulate before you react, when you turn isolation into connection, you don't just heal. You lead.

The ART of Care

Becoming True to Me

Elizabeth Moss

It's Mother's Day, 2017. I lay beside my mother in bed, listening to the steady rhythm of the oxygen machine. Its soft hum filled the room, marking each breath she took. Hospice and palliative care had supported her for nearly two years. Her breathing was practiced and intentional, she had learned how to move carefully through the final chapter of her life. She was deeply attentive to her quality of life, how she managed her breath, her anxiety, and her pain.

This was my first Mother's Day with her since I was twenty-two, and I wanted it to be special. I knew it could be my last time with her. I had flown in six times already over the past seven months, each visit carrying the same quiet thought, *Will this be the last time?*

This time felt different. I knew it might be.

I was intentional about my time with her and open to whatever healing might be possible between us. As I lay beside her, I wanted to learn from her life experience, everything I could, before she left. I was searching to hear and see her truth.

I wish I had realized this much earlier in my life. She was an independent woman with life experiences, many of which revealed who she was and her own story. During our visits, I asked questions that invited her to reflect on her life and share stories, many of which I had never heard, and some I didn't want to hear. Hearing them allowed me to see her not only as my mother, but as another woman.

I asked her softly, "Mama, what do you want me to know?"

She didn't pause or search for words.

"To radically love yourself," she said.

Her words were gentle, and they landed with surprising relevance. They didn't feel like advice. I was not able to fully absorb them at that moment. They felt like something moving through her and into me. An initiation into a way of being I had never fully allowed myself to claim, even though she had been leading the way since I was seventeen in quiet and meaningful ways. This was different.

There was no way I could understand then what or how much those words would ask of me, but something in my body recognized them deeply.

Returning Home, Not the Same

As I had experienced before in my life, my return home was not to the same life I had left. I came back to my husband of nearly three decades, my business of twenty-two years, my routines, responsibilities, and people. And yet, I was not the same woman who had boarded that plane days earlier.

The life I returned to no longer fit the woman I had become.

I tried, briefly, to settle back in to contemplate and make sense of what had happened on a day-to-day level, and how I might integrate this new awareness into my life. I didn't place my mother's words gently on a shelf to revisit later. I felt compelled to put them into practice, even though I didn't yet know how. That awareness moved with me through my work, each day, in my decisions, and in my body.

To radically love yourself.

Radical Self-Love in Action

Just two weeks after I returned home, a moment arrived that had been circling my life for years.

I had been asking for clarity quietly and internally for nearly a decade. I prayed for signs, to know when it was time to choose differently, awareness for when the right direction would become clear.

This time, the signs were loud and unmistakable.

A conflict erupted at home. He spoke words that could not be unheard, and I was told to leave. I didn't. Instead, he left. And I knew this was the moment I had been sensing and waiting for.

What surprised me most was not the fear, grief, or uncertainty, though all of that was present. What surprised me was the relief of knowing, *This is it.*

Five days later, he wanted to come back.

"I don't want you to," I said.

It was a challenge because I felt guilty. Those honest words felt terrifying and steady at the same time. I was being brave and deeply vulnerable. I was afraid, nervous, unsure, and clear.

Deep down, I knew something important was happening at that moment, and if I didn't listen to myself now, I would never be able to trust myself again. Radical self-love is not a feeling. It's a decision even when, and especially when, the decision is hard and frightening.

This was radical self-love in action.

It was what I needed. What I wanted and what I chose. It was what my mother meant.

When Life Reorganized Itself

Three months later, on my son's birthday, the phone rang.

It was a Tuesday. My ninety-three-year-old grandfather, my mother's father, had passed. He, too, had been on hospice for nearly a year. I remember everything about that moment, the light outside, the stillness, the exact moment my body absorbed the news.

The following Tuesday, my father's sister, my aunt, passed.

That morning, when my feet touched the ground as I got out of bed, something came over me. I knew I was being rebirthed. I had this sense, a message from my higher self, a feeling of peace, yet my future felt so uncertain. My life was changing at such a fast pace, and all I could do was keep reminding myself, "radically love yourself."

I spoke to my mother that week. We were all experiencing loss and grief. I finally shared with her about my marriage. She was experiencing some forgetfulness from her medications, and I didn't want to burden her. She felt sad, she said, that I didn't share this earlier.

The following Tuesday, I was in a meeting and didn't see the missed calls until I reached my car. My sister had called multiple times, and I knew that she was calling to tell me that our mother had passed. Two weeks to the day of her father.

My sister stayed on the phone with me until I made it home through traffic and heavy rain. We cried together, and I allowed myself to be supported by her. I stayed present and listened to what my body needed. When I got home, I crawled into bed to rest, be with myself, and allow myself to grieve. We called each other again and had a video call when two friends arrived to share in the final preparations and moments with my mother. It was a beautiful ceremonial experience, one I am so grateful I got to be present for.

The following Tuesday, my uncle, my aunt's husband of seventy years, passed as well, two weeks to the day after his wife.

"Oh my, what next?" I couldn't help but ask. I dreaded the next Tuesday for a few weeks, nervous about what else could possibly happen. All of my elder family members were now gone, and I felt alone.

That Thursday, my eighteen-year-old little dog, Festus, had a seizure. I held him as I let him go, knowing nothing was the same.

Everyone was gone. *What now!* I thought.

Loss after loss, the world I had known continued to fall apart and dissolve. I knew these people could have passed at any time. However, for all of them to pass within four weeks was beyond anything I could make sense of. Through it all, one sentence echoed steadily inside me: Radically love yourself.

The Responsibility Returns to Me

For most of my life, I had been responsible for someone or something.

My sister and my mother.

My marriage.

My business.

My clients.

My caregivers.

My community.

Now, one by one, those roles were completing themselves.

As a nurse, I was trained to recognize patterns, assess needs, identify problems, create plans, implement interventions, and evaluate outcomes. The nursing process is systematic, grounded, and purposeful. For decades, I applied that framework instinctively to others by assessing their needs. I diagnosed challenges and created care plans. I intervened and evaluated progress.

What I had never fully done was apply that same disciplined attentiveness to myself.

In health care, we know that unassessed pain is unmanaged pain. We know you cannot treat what you do not assess. You cannot stabilize what you refuse to acknowledge. You cannot ignore early warning signs without consequences.

For seven months, I was triaging emergencies, evaluating systems, and implementing crisis response. I knew how to assess instability in others and mobilize resources. I knew how to stabilize what was unraveling.

What I had not done was assess my own condition. I had not measured my exhaustion or depletion. I had not created a care plan for myself, and no one else was going to do that for me. Nor did anyone realize or say anything to me about this. I covered it well, and kept going.

The last thing that required my care was my business. Years earlier, in 2015, I had quietly set an intention to sell it in 2020. I would be sixty years old, and it felt like the right time.

Then the world shifted.

No one could have anticipated a global pandemic. Selling my business was the last thing on my mind as I moved fully into crisis-management mode, ensuring our elderly clients received safe care and that caregivers were supported so they could continue showing up. The healthcare system was under extraordinary strain, and frontline workers were carrying the weight of it all.

It all began before the shutdown, when Nashville was hit by a devastating tornado. A historic wind storm followed. The December before, there had been a bombing downtown. Each event required rapid response in our community, problem-solving, and calm leadership.

Then came the call I will never forget.

During the wind storm, causing much of Nashville to be without power. One of our clients whose power was out, and relied on oxygen, called and said, "I only have one hour of oxygen left."

I can still feel the chill in my body when I think about it.

There was no space for panic, only action. "What can I do? How can I help?"

I reached out to my Entrepreneurs' Organization (EO) Nashville community immediately. Within thirty minutes, two generators were secured. I drove to pick up the first one, and we could not get it started. My heart pounded, but there was no time to spiral. We pivoted and retrieved the second generator. Hospice delivered a portable oxygen tank. It was all hands on deck. We kept him breathing.

Then the order came to stay home because the pandemic was declared a state of emergency.

There was no staying home for us. We began putting a plan together for our caregivers and clients. How would we keep them safe, working, and well?

Gloves and sanitizer were nowhere to be found. Again, my EO group came through. A local distillery had an alcohol by-product from making tequila, so I purchased gallons of it. We created a station in the office and began making our own hand sanitizer. Our caregivers initially smelled like tequila until I added coconut oil and essential oils to soften it, while keeping the alcohol content high enough to kill germs.

We then formed an assembly line. We packaged kits for caregivers. We supported staff who were being pulled over and questioned about whether they were "essential" workers.

Not one public agency reached out to those of us caring for people in their homes. We were on our own. The business community showed up. Office Depot secured supplies for us. EO members stepped in repeatedly.

Home care does not stop. And for seven straight months, neither did I.

Toward the end of that shutdown season, something different happened.

It was not another crisis to manage. Instead, it was uplifting.

I was nominated for a *Nashville Business Journal* Health Care Award. That year, they introduced a new category recognizing leadership in home care, a category that had never existed before. After decades of operating quietly in the background, home care was being publicly acknowledged as essential.

During the interview, they asked what it would mean to win. At first, I almost dismissed the question. It felt cliché, but what soon came out of my mouth surprised me.

I said "It would mean that home care is finally seen as professional. That we have a seat at the healthcare table. That we are recognized as a viable, essential part of the system, not simply the hired help."

As I spoke, I realized I wasn't answering for myself alone. I was speaking for an entire sector that had worked diligently, and invisibly, for decades.

I won the award.

The category existed because of what home care demonstrated during the pandemic. We kept people safe at home when hospitals were overwhelmed. We showed up when fear was everywhere. We did not stop.

As a young Certified Nurse Technician, I remember how unseen we felt. Home care did not carry professional credibility. We did not have a seat at the table.

Now we did. It felt like closure.

The award did not change who I was, but it affirmed what I had spent my career building, turning the unseen into the seen.

Then, unexpectedly, three different people approached me about buying my business. My quiet intention was surfacing in the midst of chaos. I felt flattered, validated, and hesitant all at once. I was also exhausted, though I did not have language for that yet.

More than one person wanted what I had built, my heart, passion, and company. I followed those conversations and eventually narrowed it down to one family. That story, too, is one of healing and self-leadership, for another time.

Then, gradually, and even though it was over a year later, it felt almost suddenly, there was nothing.

No emails or calls. No fires to put out. No one needed me in the way they always had. It left a silence I had never known.

For the first time in my life, I stood in a place where my care and attentiveness could finally, completely turn inward.

It was an identity crisis. This business had been my child, and now it had grown up and moved on, guided by others.

Nothing was left, except me. Only space.

When the Care Turned Inward

Once the dust from all of the chaos of the transition settled, and I actually had time to be still, I would walk around my home, asking myself, *What do I want? What will I spend my time on, doing, how do I choose to be?*

These were new questions in so many ways. Ones that now involve no one else. It would be my life, my time, not caring for anyone but myself. *What boundaries will I need for myself?*

I recalled a time, in my younger years, as I was trying to figure out what I wanted to do when I grew up, that I floundered. I didn't want to find myself there again. *Would I? I am definitely not the same person now. I have settled into being an adult, experienced some dreams, and achieved some level of success. Now what?*

I reflected, got deeper into my body, asking questions of myself, journaling about all of this. When decisions presented themselves, I asked myself, *How did it serve me? Is it part of who I am becoming? What is the purpose for me?* So much freedom now to get to know me and really know my soul's journey and purpose!

This is how ART of Care was born. It's what I had been providing for others for my entire life, turned to me. It is the place in my soul and a process that I created as a tool that coincides with all of my pain, experiences, and purpose.

Radical Self-Love as a Way of Living

For many years, I thought self-love meant rest after depletion or a break once everything else was handled. Something earned after responsibility, perhaps a massage, a facial, or doing something nice for myself.

What I have learned instead is this: When we take care of ourselves, everyone else gets taken care of.

And it is not my responsibility to make sure they are taken care of. It is only my responsibility to make sure I am taken care of. It is the old "put the oxygen mask on yourself first, before your child" adage. This truth serves in every capacity of caring, for ourselves and for others.

Radical self-love offers a way of living that keeps us aligned, available, and whole.

The words my mother spoke did not ask me to add anything new to my life. They asked me to live differently inside the life I already had. They asked me to stop victimizing, abandoning, and oppressing myself in service to everything and everyone else.

That shift changed everything: how I lead, how I care, and how I choose.

Thank you, Mama. What a gift those words were, the greatest gift you could have ever given me. I love you more than I can ever express, and I can live out the legacy of your beautiful gift to me.

Trauma Parenting As Is

BREAKING CYCLES, BECOMING WHOLE, AND TEACHING OTHERS

Kourtney Lynn

She was revving up. She had certain tells that preceded these escalations, which often lasted for hours, leaving debris in her wake. She would henpeck her sisters, wouldn't stop when asked, like she was looking for a fight. And she was, as if she craved that kind of engagement or sensory input. This time, she was in the back seat of our pickup, driving home from a typical fifth-grade day. She had a specific smile and laugh when she was bent to upset her sisters. It turned my stomach. She was head and shoulders above her smallest sister, her decided target. Any direction only offended her sense of anarchy as she became louder, issuing threats, twisting her face, and tensing her muscles...we all knew the routine.

My own fried nervous system went into fight-or-flight, eyes narrowing on the road, heart racing, readying myself for battle. Wild instincts kick in, and it's like fighting your whole damn makeup to be a calm parent. This time, it was her little sister who responded. Her sweet six-year-old lisp rose from the back seat and formed words to describe feelings even grown-ups struggle to express, "I love you, but sometimes life is hard, and I think we need a little break." Then she stopped and cried because it was true.

That was five years ago.

Fast forward to the present. The year 2026 marked over fifteen years of nursing, eighteen years married, and six years of being a mom, something I almost gave up. Nursing wasn't my first choice. I went to college because I was supposed to. Several changes in majors later, I can fly a plane, follow apologetics, and wrap a wound. Back then, if anyone asked, all I wanted was to be barefoot and pregnant, homeschooling eight children on a micro farm. I married the man I loved, a man who was still searching, and I followed him, thinking that was my life's purpose. To follow a man.

After twelve years of trying, we had finally accepted our child-free marriage when my colleague called about three girls who needed a home. Our home. That's a long and wonderful story for another chapter. Like many affected by trauma, our girls came with invisible wounds that present with behaviors the world doesn't readily understand or tolerate well. These wounds cause a disconnect with their emotions, with their bodies, and attachment. It's no wonder that a simple request may feel like the end of the world, or a change in routine may cause the panic of the century.

Not the Enemy

Here's the kicker: Being a child's safe place allows them to express their trauma, and the kid they see at school isn't the kid showing out at home, throwing daggers at the person who might still love them when it's over. It's lonely, and it's hard. It's triggering, and too often it's reminding your own nervous system that you're safe and they're not the enemy.

There have been times, maybe too many, when I've been absolutely shook over something my kid said or did. At times, I've questioned my sanity, capacity, and life choices. In those times, more often than not, my main objective was to stop the behavior so I could feel better. I think new or well-meaning caregivers focus more on squelching the behaviors, so their kid can "survive the real world," or because the behaviors trigger something in them. Or it's just cringe. No one wants their child to feel rejected by the world.

It's more important, however, that your child doesn't feel rejected in their own home. They don't need to hide big feelings to stay loved. Otherwise, they inherit not our perfection, but our shame. When we become curious and meet the underlying need of a behavior, the behavior often dissolves on its own. And that's near impossible to do without solid, consistent, and safe authenticity.

Pretense can be scary, especially for those who are neurospicy or have a trauma-shaped brain. I feel it in those life-groups at church. My kids have a sixth sense for it. It can't be trusted, and it threatens their felt safety. They can't relax, and that nervous energy feeds unwanted behaviors. The irony is that most adults survive on pretense, perhaps unwittingly. They put on whatever mask they want the world to see, hiding whatever insecurities or anxieties they carry, and those kids can see right through it. Their mission quickly becomes to pick it apart, and it feels like a personal attack. And now, you're supposed to co-regulate, but you're trying to hold it together, and they don't trust that mask.

Allowing your kids to see you be human allows them to accept their own humanity. We're so lucky to have the plethora of trauma research available to guide parents in raising vulnerable children. We learn about Adverse Childhood Experiences, or ACEs, Trust-Based Relational Intervention (TBRI), and Attachment Theory. Ours was the pilot trauma-informed foster parenting course of Davidson County, and I'm so grateful we were equipped with these tools and concepts before our three littles came home.

"Becoming a parent will trigger every childhood trauma you have," said our counselor. If you cannot manage your own triggers and your own mask, those concepts and tools sit dusty. Talk about "co-regulation" or "connect before you correct" when your own blood is boiling. *I mean, did you hear what they just said?*

The Real Teacher

I was a really good person before kids. *Cue the laugh track.* For one thing, I did the work. Once upon a time, I was the latchkey kid of a divorced, alcoholic home that changed zip codes at least once a year. I was the oldest, left to care for my siblings or left on my own altogether. I mistook self-sacrifice for love. How many women do? I finally got angry about it in high school and decided I wasn't going to follow suit. Sorely, becoming a good person, for me, was just a very high-functioning trauma response.

Overachieving isn't the worst maladaptive coping skill. I think. My quest for wellness and self-improvement (really for control and a sense of stability) brought me to college, took me to counseling, put me in church, and had me sign marriage papers at twenty. *I cannot imagine my kid getting married at twenty, btw.* I had painful social and emotional delays to navigate in early adulthood and lots of rejection to sort through. I've carried the heartache of an insecure childhood, infertility, rejection, loss, and the aching gift of loving children I didn't carry, all with grit and a bootstrap mentality. That is to say, there was an abundance of ammunition, big red buttons for my kids to find and use against me. *"Ooo, that made her mad. Let's do that again,"* their brains say. But just like my kids, my nervous system was built for threat, not peace.

I maintained a level of stress just to feed a nervous system that feared anything different. Lots of people do. Especially those who are "too busy," those who use procrastination as a personal motivator, or the ones who "do it all" because no one else does it right. And then they blame weaponized incompetence. Sound familiar?

The bottom line is, my nervous system was teaching more than my words. Calm parenting isn't a nice sentiment; it's an effective survival strategy that takes planning and intention. I didn't grasp that part in foster training. I heard, "go learn to be calm," but I didn't hear the how. Up to fifty percent of foster homes close in the first year, mainly because of the lack of training and support (foster more.org). I would also add the lack of personal healing, but who wants to admit that? I would argue that personal healing is the only sustainable path to healing *them.* You've heard the old adage, "hurting people hurt others." Well, as you've seen, I've hurt.

> "Rock bottom became the solid foundation on which I rebuilt my life." -ACA.

At some point, my body wore thin and buckled under the weight of everything I was trying to carry nicely with bootstraps. Idiopathic IBS (a.k.a. stress gut), premature gray, insomnia, chronic fatigue, and major inflammation all became signs that I wasn't listening to my body.

I kept pushing through, "If I could just get to the other side," ...*to what?* A house that was finally finished and paid for? Increased finances to hire help? My husband was breaking down, too, and I resented him for it, for leaving me to be the strong one when I just desperately wanted to be held. My body ached because I was bone tired. Soul tired. And then, Lynnie was dying.

I hadn't seen Lynnie in over a year. She was battling cancer and had gotten to the stage where pretense didn't matter anymore. Despite her physical changes, she allowed her pictures to be posted on Facebook, and I got to watch how she wrote the rest of her story. It was beautiful. She still had that bright smile. All of her Irish red curls were gone, and her head sank into her shoulders as her spine became weaker. Lynnie traded ambition for love. She chose to love her man despite his struggles. She chose to love his children as if they came from her own womb. She showed up to all the school things, games, proms, and celebrations. She pushed her body to be present in the precious moment. Too many of us push through "just to get to the other side."

It was a gracious invitation to say goodbye. Her room at the hospice center was comfy and spacious to accommodate a good number of loved ones. I felt a bit out of place among faces I hadn't seen in a long time. God, she was beautiful, even in her last bed. Memories of our friendship before kids, when we were wild and fun and trying to figure things out, played in my head over the soft chatter in the room. Her children, all of her children, hovered with deep loyalty and love for the gift of her presence. Her solid, consistent, and safe authenticity commanded the room. I can't remember what I whispered to her, but I know I said it with tears and a prayer that she could hear them and be honored.

New Choices

I called a real estate agent on the way home. I was ready to sell everything and follow Lynnie's example. For months (maybe years?) I kept saying, "This too shall pass," until I realized it was all passing and I was going to miss it. My body, my marriage, and my family were all on the line, and we needed to make major changes to get out of a failing survival mode. We didn't need the perfect house or the idealized way of life. We needed a setup that catered to our strengths instead of challenging our weaknesses, so we could function as we are and lean into the present.

We took a personal inventory and eliminated every unnecessary responsibility we could identify, stripping our lives down to the bare minimum. It allowed healing to start, which is sometimes painful, but always good. For us, it looked like downsizing from our farmhouse to an apartment closer to all the things. And downsizing our commitments to free up our calendar for more of nothing. It was having fewer chores and more time on the couch. It was more home-cooked meals and less convenient foods, *which have their place for a spell.*

It was letting go of past relationships. It was letting go of constructs we built our marriage on. It was starting antidepressants and being intentional with daily self-care, no back-burner bullshit. It was grief, and letting myself literally sit with it for however long. It took months.

For six months, my Fitbit readiness score ranged from fifteen to forty. I learned to be patient with my body. Full burnout recovery can take anywhere from three months to a year, assuming the chronic stress is well managed. Hear me, this overhaul didn't cure our kids. Their healing may take a lifetime. It did, thankfully, give us more capacity to be the parents they need, healed (or healing), present, and better able to manage.

The Other Side

During this time, I was also working as a nurse for a detention center and group home out of Nashville. One day, this future quarterback walked in behind his social worker, six-foot-five and over three hundred pounds, six months shy of eighteen. He didn't stay long, and at one point, he asked if I'd adopt him. I looked up and held his eyes with mine. Many youth have asked if I'd adopt them. *There are youth in our backyard asking for adoption, and a few parents who can or feel capable.* Anywho, I told him the truth, that I couldn't, and he would have benefits I couldn't offer if he "aged out."

I'm sure that's a lonely, arduous journey; aging out without a mentor or guide, or the support of family. So I sat at the keys, typed my third book, and gave him the first draft. "I can't adopt you, but this is what I can offer as a mom."

It was the rough draft to *Grown-Up Basics*, a how-to guide on adulting, and it led me to Raven and Grace Press, where I met Jennifer Grace and the Clarity Catalyst program. And there it was! The missing piece to peace. I found the key to unlock TBRI, the answer to ACEs, and my new mission.

It was Jennifer who suggested I offer the Clarity Catalyst for youth. It changed my life. The 'how' I didn't grasp in the "calm-down" part of foster training became very clear. It's simple daily practices that re-wire the brain and put tools in your pocket for in-the-moment needs (or behaviors, in my case). This course would support at-risk youth, but it would also support their parents. Immensely. And this is where leadership called me, to carry "...buckets of water for those still consumed by the fire." (Stephanie Sparkles). It's where hardship and the hard-earned lessons found redemption and purpose. Today, I guide caregivers, cycle-breakers, and women who are rebuilding their lives from the inside out through retreats, coaching, and the books I write. I help people come home to themselves because becoming whole is the most generous act a parent can offer.

Healing didn't happen overnight, not for me, and I hope that's an encouragement to "trust the process." Eventually, things get easier because of the work you put into it. I'm still human. My kids still struggle. Hard days still come. And, I've learned to be steady and buoyant because I can trust myself in the waves.

I've gotten really good at modeling repair, anyway. I know how to pause instead of push. How to stay present. You see, the greatest shift wasn't in my circumstances, although we did some crazy shifts; it was in my relationship with myself. Healing helped me reclaim myself. I no longer confuse self-sacrifice with love. I no longer believe exhaustion is proof of faithfulness. I no longer perform strength while quietly falling apart. Instead, I lead from wholeness. My kids see me rest, apologize without shame, and maintain boundaries that aren't punitive. I get to give them what was lost on me; that love doesn't require disappearance. And that we can thrive now, versus surviving "to get there," *wherever that is.*

If you're parenting a troubled youth, I wrote this for you. And I'd be happy to walk alongside you. I've got a warm kitchen full of tried recipes and well-worn experiences to share. Your kids don't need perfection. Neither does your spouse. Nor do you. All they need, what the world needs, is for you to be present and content in your own authenticity. To be brave enough to name what's hard. Brave enough to ask for help. Brave enough to stop performing and start leading with truth.

And that changes everything.

⁓ℓℓ⁓

Burnout With a View

BREAKING UP WITH SURVIVAL MODE

Mladenka Dokic

This infinity bathtub sits exactly where I imagined it three years ago when I first started designing this home, a home that was supposed to be our sanctuary. Perfect treetop views, mountains on the horizon, sky for days, and the promise of northern lights dancing for me on cold winter nights. With dark cupboards and beautiful tile work, the whole room was crafted for relaxation and indulgence. A place where I would finally exhale.

Instead, I am sitting in the tub for the first time, and my only view is my infected left knee. Swollen, throbbing, and looking like it is auditioning for a medical drama. I am in a full-blown faceoff with whatever fresh hell has landed in my life. Nobody knows how the infection started or why the antibiotics refuse to touch it. The worst-case scenario is amputation. The best case is that the infection spreads downward toward my ankle instead of upward toward my groin. That is where we are at, rooting for the strategic direction of infection like it is a playoff game.

For a while, it did move toward my foot, and I cheered like a die-hard sports fan. But then it got worse. Red rings circling my leg to mark the spread. Multiple hospital trips a day to receive IV antibiotics. After a week, I refused to use crutches and hopped around on my good leg. Showing up to daycare in the morning, I looked like a deranged flamingo dropping off my kid.

Through all of this, I was home alone with my four-year-old son. My daily routine was a delightful blend of sleep deprivation, rushing to eat, and working full-time, but also chopping wood, shoveling snow, finishing the house, and raising a child with asthma who treated the ER like his personal clubhouse. We knew the emergency staff by first name, which was both nice and not something I ever wanted to know. I think I have had a handful of good sleeps since I gave birth. My job paid well, but bored a hole straight through my soul. My hair was half as thick as it used to be. Everything felt like a chore. Even blinking.

The doctors could not figure out how my knee got infected because, apparently, chronic over-functioning and living life like a one-woman survival show are not listed under causes. My entire system was cooked. My body was waving red flags while I was too busy paying bills and wiping noses to notice. My body was not whispering for help. It was staging a full mutiny. When the doctor finally discharged me with a giant shrug and no answers, it felt symbolic. I was so close. I hit the reset button but forgot to install the new operating system. Once my leg healed, I took exactly twenty-two hours off for self-care before launching myself straight back into my award-winning daily routine.

I did not know it then, but that was the beginning of years of random ailments. Once you hit your personal best with a near-amputation situation, everything else feels like a minor background character. I ignored and avoided every symptom with professional-ninja skills until I eventually ended up back in the hospital. There, with nurses constantly checking my vitals, I found comfort in the numbers. My blood pressure, temperature, pulse, and oxygen saturation were always good. The engineer in me loved the shiny screens and that my vitals were always within a good range. I felt like a thriving houseplant. My inner magpie clapped for the blinking lights as they consistently showed that nothing was wrong with me.

So, what was going on then? The lights and beeps have nothing but good news yet I'm lying in a hospital bed. In the quiet moments between the nurse's visits, somewhere between frustration, anger, exhaustion, and dread, I realized something important. There are no screens for emotional well-being. No monitor for our boundaries. No machine that beeps when we abandon ourselves. Deep down I knew something had to change in my life. I laid there and made a bullet-proof plan.

Once I got better again, I launched Operation Fix My Health. I started working out and eating unhealthily healthy. I was doing everything the physio, chiropractor, nutritionist, naturopath, doctor, friend, neighbor, and cashier at the grocery store recommended. I was convinced that if I organized my life with military precision, I would become unstoppable and never get sick like this again. Turns out living like a Navy SEAL was not sustainable for me, and to my not so surprise, surprise, I felt worse. One day, it dawned on me that instead of trying to live like I was enlisted, maybe I should sell my skills to the military and call it a day. That day, I also made my favourite cranberry pie and ate the whole thing in celebration.

The Door I Didn't Mean to Walk Through

As I was fumbling through it all, life threw me a plot twist, at no other than an Asset Management conference, which is about as glamorous as it sounds. I met a woman who would end up changing my life. We hit it off instantly. Travel, food, parenting, values, humor, all aligned. When we are together, we genuinely believe we are the funniest people alive. She is the kind of person who understands me so deeply that I do not need a filter. If you have someone like that, pause and send them a message right now to tell them how much they mean to you.

Before my long, 2,400 km road trip, she recommended a book I should listen to. Three hours into the drive, I was enjoying the narration when the book suddenly hit me with activities. Deep breath activities.

Excuse me! WTF, Christina. I wanted entertainment, not homework. *I guess I'm one of those people now that listens to self-help books and does activities,* I thought. Despite my judgments I kept listening, like the obedient student I was.

There were many activities, and after what seemed like chapter two thousand, the activity was simple: I had to describe my perfect day.

Oh, excellent, I thought, *time to lie to myself.*

My first thoughts were predictable: Sleep in, good breakfast, coffee, walk on a tropical beach, kick-ass friends, sprinkle in smoking-hot men, all with PhDs. Obviously, in this fantasy, I had a flawless body, no injuries, zero wrinkles, and could walk on my hands and do back handsprings. Then, because I had seven more hours to drive, I decided to take this seriously and expand my horizons. I had never done anything like this in my life, and by the end, I had picked out feelings, colors, relationships, smells, food, curtains, and all kinds of wonderful things. My tires were pumped, and I was giddy and smiling at the world I had created. I had a pleasant time at a gas station, picked up some snacks, checked on the car, chatted with the cashier, and used an indoor toilet.

When I hit play again, the book asked how many of those things I currently had. As I searched to make a match, I became frantic and desperate. I kept thinking and saying, *There must be something,* but the answer was that there was no match. Not one. Not even the stupid curtains.

As the tunnel vision, sweaty palms, and emotional implosion set in, I pulled over on the Cassiar Highway, turned off the engine, and put the keys on the dash. I got out of the car and started pacing up and down the shoulder, through the ditch, and in and out of the forest. My perfect-day list and my real-life were not even vague acquaintances. I realized I had spent years building a life where my needs did not exist unless someone else needed me. I had crafted a life around giving and surviving, not living. Survival mode is thrilling when you are a teenager partying with your friends. It is tragic when you find yourself over thirty, in a ditch, having a full existential meltdown.

After hours of pacing, crying, pep-talking, and briefly considering abandoning society and becoming a full-time forest creature, I went through ten stages of grief, eight stages of panic, and nine stages of personal embarrassment before I finally sat back down behind the wheel and made my decision: I am not going to participate in my own misery anymore.

The Choice I Was Not Ready For

Changing my life was slow, ugly, emotional, and deeply uncomfortable. I invented excuses that deserved awards. I told myself that wanting more out of life was selfish. That I would be seen as a bad parent, fiancé, friend, daughter, neighbor, employee, citizen, driver, everything. I reminded myself that people had it worse, which was true, but irrelevant. Pain does not stop counting because someone else has more of it or because I used to have it worse.

So, I started small and picked one thing, which was to sit down when I eat. Not save the coral reefs. Not reorganize my entire existence. Just to sit and eat. Breakfast was by far my most dysfunctional mealtime. It was a coin toss in the morning between me leaning over the counter to inhale my breakfast at record-breaking speeds or putting a breakfast sandwich in a paper towel and eating it in the car while I drove my son to daycare. I definitely stained numerous pants, shirts, and jackets with the latter method. I also realized that breakfast sandwiches are gross, but because I had not taken the time to taste my food for the last decade, how would I have known? It took four months to master breakfast. Yes, four months to be able to consistently sit down and eat a meal in the morning. This did not leave me exactly excited to make more changes, but at least I knew what I liked to eat for breakfast now.

At one point, I tried to calculate how long it would take to fix my entire life at my current rate. When in doubt, turn to math, right? I learned all that fancy math in school and have never used any of it at work, so maybe this was when my dividends were paid for five years of post-secondary education. I must have skipped the class on this kind of math because all I ended up doing was procrastinating the inevitable. I did not want to admit it at the time, but I realized this was not about scheduling or efficiency. This was about dealing with everything below the surface, the emotional iceberg I had been avoiding for decades. I tackled things one by one. Some were easy. Others took years. Some I am still working on. And there are a few I have not even started since that roadside meltdown ten years ago.

Since then, I sold the house with the fancy tub, went through a separation, and changed careers. I learned that letting go (relationships, habits, possessions, beliefs) is sometimes the healthiest thing you can do and that health, real health, is priceless. True well-being is not something you can graph or measure. It shifts, it stretches, it hides when life gets loud. It is personal in a way that numbers can never explain. It asks you to know yourself, not just manage yourself.

The Truth I Didn't Want to See

After working with hundreds of people, I learned that I am not alone. Far from it, actually. We all want fewer days where we're treading water with our chin barely above the surface, and more days where breathing doesn't feel like a skill we forgot to practice. More days where the person in the mirror looks familiar instead of like a stranger who's clearly been through some things. We're not chasing perfect lives. We're chasing lives that genuinely feel like ours. Lives we're present for, not just managing like an unpaid intern who never clocks out.

Life doesn't get better because it gets easier. That's a lie sold in very convincing fonts. Life gets better the moment you decide you're done with the bullshit. The moment you stop waiting for unicorns, signs, or a laminated permission slip and give yourself a quiet, unapologetic yes. Not the fireworks, yes. Not the social media-worthy, yes. The shaky, inconvenient, *I guess I'm doing this,* yes. That first honest yes on the side of the highway changed everything for me. It cracked the door to a new story, one that finally felt like it belonged to me. And NO.B.S. became the tool I use to keep writing it.

So what does NO.B.S. actually look like in real life? It's not dramatic. There's no montage. It looks like drawing a line in the sand and stepping over it. You can glance back. That's human. But you don't walk back. Why would you? Look at everything you've already survived. The late nights. The self-doubt. The way you carried far more than was ever yours to hold. You didn't go through all of that just to stay the same.

This is where NO.B.S. lives. As a backbone, not on a poster or mug. If you want a mug, go get one, but it will eventually fall off the counter and shatter, much like your feelings already have. Save yourself the cleanup. Drink your coffee out of whatever mug you own, preferably the one hiding in the back of the cupboard that says, "I'm smokin' hot." Look at it. Smile. Then get back to work.

There is no rescue coming, perfect timing, or magic fix. Just you, showing up, taking responsibility, and deciding your life gets to feel like it belongs to you. That decision, made imperfectly and on repeat, is how you stop surviving and enjoy the view.

And if you're reading this from so deep in the rabbit hole that change feels like a fairy tale for other people, borrow my belief. I believe in you even if you don't yet. You are worthy. You are talented. You are beautiful in the real, human, been-through-it way. You don't need a plan or confidence. NO.B.S. asks for one thing only.

A step.

The Year I Stopped

A New York Hustler Learns to Live Like the Rest of the World

Jennifer Grace

If you're wondering what kind of woman I am, I'll make it easy. I'm a double Capricorn, New York born, and raised in a household where "overachieving" wasn't a personality trait, it was the wallpaper.

I'm an only child. And no, my hustle wasn't born out of needing acceptance or applause. It was literally what I watched.

My mother was a mover, a shaker, a name-taker. She was building women's centers across all five boroughs of New York alongside women like Gloria Steinem, creating real-life spaces for peace, empowerment, and protection. She was out there building an empire of impact while raising me and getting her master's degree from NYU. Like it was casual.

My father, who my mom divorced when I was seven, was the managing director at Cantor Fitzgerald, overseeing hundreds of bond brokers and billions of dollars. The kind of world where "rest" is something other people do.

So when people ask me why I became a high-functioning lunatic with a color-coded calendar and a deep suspicion of naps, the answer is simple.

Hustle was a family language.

That was normal to me and the air I breathed.

That was the definition of adulthood I witnessed.

And yes, I loved the adrenaline. I loved the dopamine of checking boxes. I loved the identity of "the woman who can do it all." I wasn't trying to prove I was worthy. I already assumed I was. I just thought this was what you do when you're alive. You execute. You keep it moving.

New York trained me well and Miami fueled it when I moved there. And the coaching world? Oh honey, that was like handing a Type A Capricorn a megaphone and a mission. More clients. More launches. More stages. More impact. More notifications. More proof.

Rest was something you earned after you crushed it. Even then, rest was suspicious.

I'd sit on the couch like a guilty criminal, scrolling my phone and thinking about what I should be doing. I would "relax," but only while strategizing. I'd take a bath while answering emails. I'd do yoga, but only if it counted.

If productivity was a religion, I was a preacher.

Then COVID-19 happened.

The world stopped.

And for the first time in my adult life, I did too.

Beyond the Checklists

All the external noise that kept my nervous system in fight-or-flight got turned down overnight. No packed calendar. No constant movement. No more dog and pony show.

Just...stillness.

At first, that stillness felt like withdrawal, like someone took away my drug and expected me to be fine. I didn't know what to do with the empty space. I didn't know who I was without the constant "next thing." I didn't know how to be with myself without turning it into a project, workshop, or retreat.

So naturally, I tried to hustle my way through slowing down.

I made schedules for my rest and goals for my nervous system. I tried to optimize peace. I was basically like, "Okay, serenity, let's circle back by Thursday."

Then something surprising happened.

Under the silence, I started to hear myself. What I heard was, "You're exhausted, not lazy."

Exhausted in the deeper way of overstimulated, overextended, over-responsible, and under-rested for so long that I thought tension was normal. I realized I wasn't failing at life. I was carrying a system inside my body that never allowed me to fully exhale. And once you notice that, you can't un-notice it.

Around that time, my boyfriend Sev and I did something that shocked even me. We sold everything and became digital nomads for two-and-a-half years.

Yes, we did the thing.

We sold the stuff and packed the suitcases. We released the clutter and walked away from the predictable. And for a Capricorn, that is basically a controlled burn.

Here's what made it work: we didn't travel like we were chasing a highlight reel. We traveled like we were building a new nervous system.

We rented Airbnbs for four months at a time, long enough to actually live in a place and not just visit.

Four months on the beach in Saint Augustine.

Four months on a lake surrounded by mountains in North Carolina.

Four months on the sea in Mallorca, Spain.

During those trips, I collected evidence that there are other ways to live because the more we lived in different places, the more I noticed something that felt almost offensive to my Capricorn programming. Other cultures were not worshipping exhaustion. They were not acting like rest was a guilty pleasure. They were not living like humans were machines built for output. They treated rest like a normal part of being alive.

At first, my American brain was horrified. *How does anything get done if people aren't constantly proving they deserve to exist?*

Spoiler: things get done.

Just not at the expense of everyone's nervous system.

Spain gave me back my afternoons.

Germany taught me boundaries I didn't know were allowed.

And the Dutch handed me a permission slip to do...nothing.

Spain: Where Rest Is Just a Tuesday

Mallorca was where my nervous system met its match. The ocean. The light. The slower pace. The way people ate meals like they weren't being chased.

And then there was the *siesta*.

Now, Americans love to romanticize *siestas* like it's just a cute European thing. But when you're living there, you realize it's a rhythm. In the afternoon, the energy changes as shops close and streets quiet down. The heat makes everyone soften, and the day has a built-in exhale.

They call it slow living. I loved that.

The first time I truly noticed it, my inner Capricorn had a full body reaction.

"What do you mean we're pausing in the middle of the day?"

"What do you mean we're not grinding through the afternoon slump with caffeine and spite?"

"What do you mean we're honoring the fact that humans get tired?"

But then I tried it. I stopped fighting my natural dip in energy and rested.

What happened next was clarity. My brain stopped buzzing. My body stopped bracing. My creativity returned like a friend I'd neglected. And I realized something no one taught me in hustle school.

Sometimes you don't need a new strategy. Sometimes you need a nap.

Germany: The Holy Sabbath of Quiet

Then we spent time in places that introduced me to a concept I wish came with a passport, collective rest.

Germany has a tradition of quiet time and Sundays that are sacred. Shops closed, loud activities are discouraged. A cultural agreement that says, "Today is not for noise."

Imagine that.

A whole society that doesn't treat Sunday like "catch up on errands and punish yourself for not being productive." German Sundays are for family, nature walks, leisurely meals, museums, and relaxing at home. It's not self-care content. It's just life.

And what hit me wasn't only the quiet, it was the permission because in the U.S., rest often feels like a private negotiation. You have to fight for it, justify it, or defend it. But in cultures with built-in rest, you don't have to be the lone soldier protecting your peace. The culture protects it.

In Germany, I watched people take slow walks without headphones. I watched families eat like they had nowhere else to be. I watched the day unfold without urgency.

And I thought, *Oh my God. This is what a regulated nervous system looks like.*

So I made my own version.

I started creating a "German Sunday" at home. No errands that could wait. No projects disguised as relaxation. No cleaning spree that was actually anxiety in a headband.

Just presence.

A walk, long meal, book. Quiet.

And the world didn't end. No one revoked my ambition, and my clients didn't disappear. The only thing that disappeared was the constant internal pressure.

The Netherlands: The Art of Doing Nothing Without Dying Inside

Then I met my final boss: Niksen, the Dutch art of intentionally doing nothing.

Not meditation or mindfulness.

Not "rest with a goal."

Not "self-care that you can monetize later."

Nothing.

No outcome.

No productivity.

No improvement plan. Just allowing your mind to wander and your body to exist.

When I first heard about it, my Capricorn brain tried to file a formal complaint. *Excuse me, what is the purpose of doing nothing?*

And the Dutch are basically like, "There is no purpose. That's the point."

This was deeply confronting because hustle culture trains us to believe that if we're not doing something, we're wasting time. And if we're wasting time, we're wasting our life. And if we're wasting our life, we're failing.

Niksen doesn't care. Niksen is like, "Sit. Stare. Daydream. Be human."

So I tried it in small doses, with five minutes on my porch without my phone.

Then ten minutes looking at the water without turning it into a caption. A quiet cup of coffee without scrolling. Sitting in a chair and letting my thoughts drift like clouds.

At first, it felt like I was breaking a rule.

Then it felt like I was coming home because I learned that doing nothing is not nothing. It's nervous system repair. It's creative recovery. It's a rebellion against the idea that your worth is measured in output.

What Changed in My Real Life

I did not become a permanently serene woman who floats through life in linen. I'm still a Capricorn. I still like building things and love momentum. I still get excited by a plan.

And my ambition was never powered by anxiety. It was powered by what I grew up witnessing, big vision, real leadership, and the belief that you build what matters. The difference now is *how* I build. I'm not building on caffeine, pressure, and constant motion. I'm building from rhythm, regulation, and a life that actually feels like mine.

And that changed everything.

I stopped scheduling my life around my ego and started scheduling it around my energy.

I stopped treating rest like a reward and started treating it like a requirement.

I stopped believing urgency was a personality trait.

I stopped glamorizing exhaustion.

I stopped calling "busy" a compliment.

And I started noticing a few things:

When I rest, I make better decisions.

When I slow down, I hear my intuition.

When I stop over-driving, I create more.

When I protect my peace, I become a better leader.

When I stop performing productivity, I start enjoying my life.

And here's the part that will annoy the hustlers: I actually got more done because I stopped burning my body to the ground trying to outrun time.

I started building from flow. That's a very different engine.

Hustle makes you feel like you're always behind.

Flow makes you feel like you're in a relationship with time.

Hustle says, "Do more."

Flow says, "Do what matters."
Hustle says, "Prove it."
Flow says, "Live it."

The Truth I Didn't Want to Learn

If you're a high-achieving woman who secretly doesn't know how to stop, I see you.

You're competent and responsible. Capable. The one people count on. You might even be the one who holds the whole family system together. You're the woman who can do everything until your body says, "We're done."

And here's my no-BS truth. The hustle is not your identity.
It's your conditioning.
It's what you learned to do because it was normal and rewarded.
It's what you learned to do because it worked, until it didn't.

COVID forced me to confront that. Travel confirmed it, and slow living healed it. Not all at once, but enough that I can say that rest is not what happens after you finish your life. Rest is part of how you live it.

Here's what surprised me most: Slow living made me less insane. My creativity came back like a cat who had been hiding under the bed during a house party. My body stopped bracing. My relationships got sweeter because I wasn't talking to people while mentally replying to emails. I stopped "relaxing" the way I used to, which was basically doing admin work in cute pajamas. And yes, I still have moments where my inner New Yorker shows up like, *We're wasting daylight!* When that voice gets loud, I do what any emotionally mature woman would do and negotiate. I don't try to kill my ambition. I just stop letting it drive the car.

I used to think my value was measured by output. Now I think my value is measured by how present I am for my life. I still want big things. I still build big things. I just refuse to sacrifice my nervous system on the altar of somebody else's productivity standards. That, to me, is how I healed to lead.

At the Edge of Capacity

INVISIBLE ACTS OF LEADERSHIP

Sage Stevens

In Los Angeles, the expectation is not just competence but ease—everyone is meant to be "fabulous." Pain has no obvious place in that performance. Admitting pain, especially the kind that consumes energy, patience, and composure, rarely fits the script. There are moments when simply standing, smiling, and engaging requires deliberate effort: leaning on a table for support, managing discomfort quietly, sustaining conversation long enough to form a meaningful connection, and hoping that moment carries professional weight.

Living inside that expectation taught me something no mentor ever could. Leadership is not tested in moments of ease, but at the edge of what the body can sustain, at the edge of capacity.

Health recalibrates leadership in a way no mentor ever could. It removes the illusion that availability equals value. A health crisis clarifies which demands are essential and which are simply loud. Recovery, I discovered, is not returning to who you were before. It's becoming precise about who you can be sustainably and for how long.

The most consequential leadership decision I ever made was what I stopped being available for. There comes a point when pushing through stops being resilient and starts being self-betrayal. That point is where leadership actually begins.

Leadership rarely announces itself at the beginning. More often, it arrives at the edge of what you can no longer endure. For me, that decision arrived through my physical body and mental well-being. I learned that resilience has a shelf-life when it's fueled by disregard rather than care. The margin that once absorbed that tradeoff was gone. I couldn't maintain it. I tried for over two years, and I was exhausted. I kept asking myself how long my recovery was supposed to take, whether I had the stamina, grit, and wherewithal to reach the other side.

When I truly listened to my body and intuition, it became clear that I would never return to my former self. But I did believe I could improve beyond where I was, and I held on to that. You can negotiate expectations. You can push through discomfort for a while. Eventually, both the body and the culture you move through impose limits you cannot override.

What changed was not my ambition, but my willingness to stay in places that required me to divide myself to keep going, places where there was no room for all of me. Only later did I recognize this moment for what it was, the beginning of a powerful pivot in my life.

Pain Demands Endurance

Pain demands planning every step, every exit, every hour.

Wholeness allows ease, and freedom doesn't require calculation.

When your body requires extra care, every decision sharpens. There is a painstaking amount of thought that goes into planning each day to minimize unnecessary exertion and the pain it produces.

Will my wardrobe choice be a regret later as I grow weary and the pain escalates? Will I need to bring a change of wardrobe with me?

Initially, I needed to adapt as I could barely walk, and still struggle today, but it will take more than a health crisis to make me relinquish my sense of style. That also causes people to doubt that I have any health conditions. When you look composed and well-dressed, most people assume that you are a normal, healthy functioning individual. I wish when I was out in public I could bleed from a cut--that way people would have a visual indication that I am dealing with an issue. Instead, when you appear, more less, an average human, people have no idea that you are doing everything in your power to maintain composure in public settings, when on the inside you feel like you are being electrocuted from the inside out.

Over time, you stop entertaining avoidable friction and over-explaining. You stop participating in dynamics that extract more than they return. There were things I had to leave because they were incompatible with the life I intended to lead next.

Invisible leadership load is the cumulative, unrecognized work of regulating pain, managing perception, and sustaining function so systems do not have to adapt.

Pain is more common than we admit. Many manage quietly because it would disrupt expectations they cannot afford to negotiate. So pain becomes private; professionalism absorbs the cost, and leadership proceeds as if capacity were neutral. It isn't.

This is the invisible leadership load. What looks like composure is often leadership energy spent on containment rather than direction. Living this way trains a particular kind of leadership, one built on anticipation, restraint, and constant self-regulation. The load increases when performance is mistaken for capacity and access is assumed to be limitless. Over time, leadership suffers from the fragmentation required to remain acceptable. Nothing breaks, nothing shows, and the cost remains hidden.

With people I trust, I allow the truth—the fatigue, brain fog, limitations, and accommodations required to make the day possible. But in public, professionally and socially, I perform. I do not explain the effort. On difficult days, if I need to be present, the pain may show, and sometimes that visibility carries a cost. Oftentimes, empathetic or observant people can sense when something is wrong.

Silence about pain leads others to assume I have more to give than I do. Especially when, to the outside world, I appear composed. I love fashion. I love shoes. I was a competitive figure skater and a spokesmodel, so being put together has always mattered to me. I competed on broken blisters and bleeding toes, so I have a high pain threshold. My current injury soon made my prior foray as an athlete a vital experience in what I was to face.

What I do not yet know is what does it cost to keep surviving in silence?

Adaption and Survival

Many people living with invisible conditions become experts at this without ever choosing it.

You learn how to conserve energy without being seen. How to remain competent and engaged while negotiating discomfort internally. Society tends to avoid conflict. I do not. I do not have the energy to explain myself over and over, and I stopped doing so. I choose self-respect over appeasement.

Living this double life becomes unsustainable because the fragmentation does. Being one person in private and another in public requires constant translation. Leadership suffers when too much effort goes into managing perception instead of making decisions.

For a long time, I believed this was simply the price of continuing. I told myself it was professionalism. Strength. Grace under pressure. What I didn't realize was how much leadership energy was being spent on concealment rather than direction. Living this way trains you to read rooms differently. You become acutely aware of environments that demand performance over presence. Of expectations that assume limitless access. Of cultures that reward stamina and penalize honesty.

Eventually, this awareness forces a reckoning. This is where leaving becomes necessary.

I stopped showing up at times because I physically could not do it, and then, the other times, I stopped showing up where it required erasing a part of myself to be accepted. The shift was subtle yet decisive. I began choosing spaces where my leadership did not depend on pretending capacity I did not have that day.

What changed was my permission to lead without constant self-editing.

There is strength in privacy, but there is also authority in alignment. When internal reality and external leadership are no longer at odds, clarity can return. Energy consolidates. Decisions become cleaner.

What rarely gets named in this double life is the additional work it requires. The strain is being asked to let go before the next life has taken shape. The question then becomes: When can I fully let go of the old version of myself? I hold onto it until I understand what the next version requires because letting go without orientation feels less like growth and more like erasure.

If a transformation is required, it will have to be honest. Like a caterpillar, I will need to go inward before I emerge, and whatever comes out of the cocoon must be able to sustain the life ahead.

The Invisible Labor of Leadership

Much of leadership work is visible by design. Decisions, outcomes, presence—these are the markers we recognize and reward. But there is another layer of labor that rarely enters leadership conversations because it happens quietly.

Invisible labor is the work required to remain functional in systems that assume capacity is neutral. It is the ongoing effort of calibration, such as monitoring energy, anticipating strain, planning exits, regulating tone, and managing perception, all while continuing to contribute at a high level.

Invisible labor does not appear on calendars. It is not measured, acknowledged, or compensated, but it shapes every decision.

Research in cognitive neuroscience and pain psychology has shown that ongoing pain competes for attentional and executive resources, increasing cognitive load even when outward performance remains unchanged.[1] What looks like ease from the outside is often the result of continuous internal calculation, attention divided between the task at hand and the management of the body performing it. Over months and years without a clear timeline for recovery, that strain becomes impossible to ignore.

For leaders operating under constraint, leadership also involves constant assessment. How long can I stay? What will the ramifications of this be? What will recovery from this exertion require? These calculations happen beneath conversations that appear fluid and effortless on the surface.

This labor is frequently misread as personality. Careful planning is mistaken for rigidity. Early exits are labeled impatience. Restraint is interpreted as a lack of ambition. In reality, these behaviors are strategies developed in response to finite capacity.

Invisible labor intensifies in environments that reward stamina over sustainability. For example, when availability becomes a proxy for commitment. In such systems, individuals absorb strain privately, so the environment does not have to change.

Occupational psychology research on emotional labor and suppression shows that concealing strain requires sustained physiological regulation, even when outward behavior remains composed.[2] Over time, this regulation carries measur-

---

1. Eccleston, C., & Crombez, G. (1999). Pain demands attention: A cognitive–affective model of the interruptive function of pain. Psychological Bulletin, 125(3), 356–366. — Foundational research demonstrating that pain competes for attentional and executive resources.

2. Gross, J. J., & Levenson, R. W. (1997). Hiding feelings: The acute effects of inhibiting negative and positive emotion. Journal of Abnormal Psychology, 106(1), 95–103. Hochschild, A. R. (1983). The Managed Heart: Commercialization of Human Feeling. — Foundational work on emotional labor and the physiological cost of suppression.

able cognitive and physical tolls, contributing to fatigue, depletion, and reduced decision quality. The impact of invisible labor accumulates quietly. By the time it becomes visible, through disengagement, withdrawal, or burnout, the damage has already occurred.

Research on burnout consistently demonstrates that exhaustion is driven less by workload alone and more by sustained misalignment: the ongoing effort required to compensate for systems that do not reflect live reality.[3] High performers are particularly vulnerable because they are more likely to carry unacknowledged compensatory load.

This is why capable leaders often leave without spectacle or explanation. They exit because they have been subsidizing assumptions that were never true about their capacity, availability, and neutrality of the body. They have been doing the work required to keep systems appearing functional, at personal cost. The irony is that invisible labor often masquerades as competence. The more effectively someone manages constraint without complaint, the less visible the burden becomes.

When too much effort goes into managing perception, less remains for discernment, creativity, and long-range thinking. Leadership then shifts from intentional to reactive. Invisible labor accumulates until a decision becomes unavoidable such as continuing compensating for the system with your health and attention, or redesign your participation with it.

Naming this labor matters to reclaim agency. You stop agreeing to norms that quietly extract from you. You become selective about where your energy goes. You begin measuring return not in optics or endurance, but in sustainability and alignment.

This is where our power returns.

---

3. Maslach, C., & Leiter, M. P. (2016). Understanding the burnout experience: Recent research and its implications for psychiatry. World Psychiatry, 15(2), 103–111. — Burnout linked to values and role misalignment rather than workload alone.

Research across pain science, occupational health, and organizational psychology converges on the same truth that bodies are not interchangeable instruments, and systems that pretend otherwise externalize their burdens onto the individual.[4] When leaders stop absorbing those costs silently, they become more precise. This precision is what allows leadership to last.

Leaving Room

Leaving is not abandonment; it is the creation of conditions under which leadership can remain intact. Leaving room is how coherence is restored when capacity has been misread as availability.

I've learned to leave before I'm expected to. What people might casually call an "Irish goodbye" is, for me, a practiced form of self-governance. When possible, I leave the event, meeting, or room when I reach my physical capacity before my pain spikes into something harder to manage.

Through this, I've learned that only a small portion of any room does the real work. A few conversations carry meaning. Staying for the remaining stretch rarely adds value; it only increases the burden. However, knowing when you've already received what mattered most is where the value lies.

Physical limits, when ignored, rarely stay physical. They can erode composure, and composure, in public leadership settings, requires more stamina than most people realize. Leaving at the right moment preserves my clarity and everyone else's. It allows me to remain measured, professional, and intact, rather than resilient in ways that quietly extract too much.

Leaving room is a disciplined act of authorship. When you choose what no longer belongs in your next chapter, you protect the integrity of what comes

---

4. Job Demands–Resources (JD-R) Model: Demerouti et al. (2001). The job demands–resources model of burnout. Journal of Applied Psychology, 86(3), 499–512. — Demonstrates how unacknowledged demands externalize cost onto individuals.

next before it has to defend itself. This is how leadership matures. Leaving room also recognizes that only a small portion of what we participate in actually carries meaning. The rest is often noise, familiar, socially rewarded, and quietly expensive.

Most people don't give their power away all at once. They give it away incrementally, by staying too long in rooms where their contribution has already been made and continuing conversations that have stopped evolving. By honoring expectations that no longer align with the person they are becoming.

When you leave at the right moment, you preserve energy for what actually compounds by protecting your attention and foresight. Leaving room also creates space for others. When you don't overstay, you don't dominate. When you step back deliberately, you allow new leadership to surface. This is especially true when capacity is finite. When health, care, or constraint is part of the system, every unnecessary demand carries weight. Leaving room becomes a way of honoring reality rather than fighting it and staying in a relationship with your future self.

Responsible Recovery

The quietest leadership decision I made was to stop treating recovery as a temporary interruption and start treating it as a governing principle. Once health became non-negotiable, everything else reorganized itself accordingly: work, relationships, pace, and even identity.

What surprised me most was that the less I explained my boundaries, the more effective they became. I resented that I still looked mostly the same, maybe some added weight because of limited mobility, and on really bad flare-up days, my hair would be affected, and I had to prevent myself from giving myself a haircut. Still, I resented that there were no significant visible imperfections for the average person to notice that justified the limits I now lived with.

Because I looked "fine," people expected me to act fine. In the first three years, that expectation proved hard to meet. The pain itself is all-consuming combined with the exhaustion from trying to meet assumptions that no longer match my reality. At first, I wanted to communicate with others, so I explained and clarified. I offered facts. Over time, I realized that many people were less interested in understanding than in preserving who they believed me to be.

Eventually, I stopped negotiating perception. I stated what was true, my experience, and allowed others to interpret it as they want, without adjusting my behavior to secure their belief. If I reach my capacity for walking, I use crutches. If sitting upright becomes intolerable, I sit on the floor. I no longer perform composure or continuity to protect anyone else's comfort. Pain has a way of stripping what is unnecessary. When I stopped explaining and began acting in alignment with my capacity, my boundaries became unmistakable.

There are days when I appear outwardly composed, yet my mobility is constrained, and other days when I cannot get off the couch. Mornings are always the hardest. What I have learned is that resilience is sometimes built in invisibility. When you rise from pain with empathy and intention, true leadership is embodied.

That shift is supported by daily practices: meditation that steadies my attention, somatic breathing that helps regulate pain disruption, red light therapy that allows healing without medication, and daily chants and affirmations that keep my mind from racing when my body is already taxed.

The most important leadership decision I made was to stop treating recovery as a temporary interruption. At about the three-year mark, I realized that the person I was was no longer available to me. That reckoning came with clarification of what my life was to be, and from then on, I was not going to apologize for what I needed to maintain my comfort and prevent flare-ups. Some people adapted and tolerated. Some drifted away. Others, with empathy to stay, remained.

When you honor your capacity, you protect your future contribution. You lead without burning the very instrument required to continue. When you choose what no longer belongs in your next chapter, you protect the integrity of what comes next.

And clarity, once earned this way, is not something you give back.

Take what resonates and leave what doesn't. Trust the part of you that knows what you need because instinct exists for survival, and ignoring it has consequences.

My Hands Found a Voice

THE STORY MY BODY REFUSED TO KEEP SILENT

Eren Torres

Have you ever wondered what all women have in common? Regardless of our backgrounds, the countries we come from, the values we inherit, the challenges we face, or the family dynamics we are born into and silently agree to carry in this lifetime, our differences seem louder than the similarities.

Different languages.

Different accents.

Different histories.

Different mothers.

Different wounds.

And yet, when I sit with women long enough, when the urgency of explaining fades, when the nervous system softens, when the body no longer feels the need to defend itself, something unmistakable rises.

A quiet recognition.

A shared exhaustion.

A feeling of being seen without having to justify pain.

Inside every human being, two forces are always present: feminine and masculine. One receives. One holds. One senses. One structure. One feels. One protects. When they are balanced, we feel grounded, intuitive, and capable of rest. When one is silenced or containment is absent, the body finds another way to communicate.

Sometimes, it speaks through illness.

My Body Learned Before I Could Speak

I grew up in a small town where tradition was safety and silence was loyalty. It was a place where emotions were managed privately, if at all. Anxiety did not exist. Depression was not named. Pain was something you endured quietly and learned not to discuss.

Within the first seven years of life, the most critical period of nervous system development, my own process of becoming was interrupted. Before I had the chance to discover who I was, I learned how to contain someone else.

My mother lived with an undiagnosed borderline personality disorder. At the time, there was no framework for it or protection from it, only emotional shifts that came without warning. One day, the house was full of energy and intensity. The next, it was heavy, silent, unpredictable.

So, I adapted.

I learned how to read faces before words. How to sense danger before sound.

How to regulate someone else's emotions before I had permission to feel my own.

This is how my nervous system was trained.

Long before Premenstrual Dysphoric Disorder (PMDD) entered my vocabulary, my body already lived in cycles of anticipation, collapse, and recovery. Long before hormones were blamed, my system had learned that rest was unsafe.

PMDD arrived like a memory my body refused to forget. Every month, my emotions would surge without warning. Energy would disappear from my limbs.

My thoughts would darken and distort. I would feel unfamiliar inside my own body, as if someone else had taken over my mind and voice.

I tried to silence it by saying,

"Be stronger."

"Push through."

"Act normal."

I repeated these phrases as survival strategies. I learned how to smile while unraveling inside. I showed up to work while my body felt like it was shutting down and doubted myself when the symptoms felt overwhelming.

But the body does not whisper forever.

PMDD grew louder each year because my body was tired of being ignored. Tired of translating survival into symptoms no one wanted to hear.

If you live with PMDD, you know the moment.

The moment you question your sanity.

The moment you fear yourself.

The moment you wonder if this version of you will take over permanently.

I was there.

And then I left my country.

When Everything Split

I was twenty-two years old, three months away from graduating from a private university. My future felt almost assembled. Then, in a matter of weeks, everything collapsed. My sexuality was exposed before I was ready. My sense of belonging fractured. My family's support disappeared.

So I moved to Oklahoma City for what was meant to be only a two-week vacation. Instead it turned into a nightmare, as immigration became mere survival.

Inside the factory, most of us lived under false names. Social Security numbers were rented like currency. Exploitation disguised as opportunity. Supervisors knew. They always knew. I remember the day they offered me the job. A manager pulled me aside, his voice low, almost kind. He said they were doing me a favor.

They knew I didn't have papers. They knew the work was illegal for them and for me, but he framed it as protection.

Hypervigilance became constant. My body stayed braced, waiting for discovery, punishment, rejection. PMDD intensified. Hormones do not regulate well inside fear, and cycles do not soften when the nervous system never rests.

Survival as an immigrant taught my body urgency.

Every day felt like running.

Every night felt like a collapse.

The machines exploited the people inside them. The most dangerous role on the factory floor. No safety training. No insurance. If something happened, it would be on me. They paid less than the minimum they could legally get away with, saving every dollar they would have owed an American worker.

Within the first six months, nearly eighty percent of us were injured. Spinal pain was so severe that some could barely walk. Hands swollen and burning, between extreme heat and extreme cold. I still feel it in my arms when I enter cold rooms. Bodies were breaking faster than anyone admitted. We couldn't go to the hospital. Fear of deportation kept us silent, so we endured the pain until it passed or until we were forced to return to our countries, disabled, our bodies spent.

I remember the day an ICE raid swept through the factory. Someone shouted a warning, and instinct took over. I climbed inside a metal toolbox and pulled my knees to my chest. The air was thin. My breath stayed shallow. My muscles locked in place, afraid even the sound of breathing would give me away.

Hours passed. I listened as people were taken. Voices disappeared. Doors closed. Eventually, the machines started again, and those who remained returned to work as if nothing had happened.

That night, when I finally stepped outside, the parking lot was empty. No phone. No ride. No proof I existed.

What Happened to Me?

I worked multiple jobs. Some days meant long shifts at the factory and four hours at a coffee shop. On weekends, I took a third job at a fast-food restaurant. There were no days off, only transitions from one kind of exhaustion to another.

The factory was a workout disguised as labor. In twelve hours, we were allowed two fifteen-minute breaks to use the bathroom only with permission and one ten-minute break to eat. The line never slowed. Heavy plastic water pipes, larger than my own body, came at me one after another, relentless. I had seconds to trim them, lifting and cutting with a strength I didn't know I possessed. My body learned speed because survival demanded it.

At the restaurant, my hands burned as I reached again and again toward the hot cooking plates, just as I had struggled at the factory, five feet tall, unable to reach the higher levels, forcing my body to stretch beyond its limits. By the end of the night, my hands smelled like burned hair.

With time, most of the marks faded. I carry only two scars now.

A pivotal moment came when I reached the bottom. I could not be more humiliated, more emptied, more erased.

And then, beneath the noise, a soft voice rose inside me. *You were not born for this, it said. You are meant for more.*

It felt less like a thought and more like remembering something ancient, buried in my body. A sacred voice from my deepest consciousness whispered that no sacrifice was ever made so I could live in fear and degradation, but so I could live in dignity, abundance, and truth.

That was the moment I understood that my pain was not a flaw. My suffering was a signal. And I deserved a life that did not require me to keep betraying myself to survive.

From Resistance to Regulation

For a long time, I believed healing meant making the symptoms stop. I believed it meant silencing the chaos, calming the storm, fixing what felt broken inside me. I searched for relief with urgency, desperation, and fear. Every month, when PMDD arrived, it felt like a personal failure, as if my body were betraying me, as if all the work I had done meant nothing if I still collapsed into darkness.

I lived in resistance. Resistance to my body. Resistance to my emotions. Resistance to the version of myself that appeared every cycle and refused to behave.

I fought my body with discipline, logic, and force. I tried to outthink it, override it, dominate it. I told myself I had survived worse. Immigration. Loss. Exile. Fear. *If I could survive those things*, I told myself, *I should be able to survive a few days a month.*

When ICE raided the factory, I hid inside a metal toolbox. I made myself small. I didn't move. I didn't breathe deeply. I didn't exist. That toolbox became my only safety, four metal walls that taught my body one rule, disappear to stay alive.

Years later, PMDD asked for the same thing.

When the symptoms arrived, my mind reached for the same survival strategy. I withdrew and went quiet. I stopped trusting my thoughts, my voice, my presence. Emotionally, I climbed back into that toolbox, freezing, hiding, waiting for the danger to pass, because my nervous system had learned that visibility meant risk.

But PMDD does not respond to force. It responds to safety.

I did not know that yet.

At first, healing looked like exhaustion. It looked like admitting I could no longer do this alone. It looked like sitting across from therapists and doctors, trying to put language to something that lived far deeper than words. Trauma lives in our body, hiding in breath patterns, muscle tension, hormonal cascades, and nervous-system loops that fire before thought ever arrives.

Talk therapy gave me awareness, but awareness alone did not regulate my body. That was one of the hardest truths to accept.

When trauma is layered with childhood emotional responsibility, identity suppression, immigration survival, and chronic fear, conversation alone cannot untangle it. The body must be invited into the process, slowly, gently, and repeatedly.

Eye Movement Desensitization and Reprocessing (EMDR) was one of the first moments my nervous system felt seen. Memories that had lived as sensations, tight chest, nausea, dissociation, and collapse, finally had a pathway to move. I did not have to relive everything, and my body already remembered. EMDR allowed those memories to complete cycles that had been interrupted by survival. What once felt like a constant threat slowly began to feel like something in the past.

Medication followed as support. This was a reframe I had to learn.

For years, I resisted medication because I believed healing meant doing it "naturally," on my own, without help. But regulation is not about pride; it is about capacity. There were moments when my nervous system was so dysregulated that expecting it to self-correct was unrealistic and cruel.

Medication gave my body a pause in which my system could remember what balance felt like long enough for me to build skills around it. Medication gave me space to respond to my emotions instead of drowning inside them.

Let me clarify. I am not a doctor. I deeply respect every person's journey, every body, every nervous system, and every path toward healing. This is not an invitation to choose medication over natural approaches, nor is it an argument against them. I have always believed in addressing the root rather than masking the surface, and I continue to believe that a regulated, conscious lifestyle is foundational to healing.

At the same time, I feel a responsibility to speak honestly.

In my search for healing, I encountered books and teachings that strongly encouraged abandoning medication and treating chronic conditions solely through will, mindset, or spirituality. For me, this was not only confusing; it was dangerous. I pushed myself relentlessly to be "natural," to avoid labels and the unspoken stigma of being someone "on antidepressants." I did not want my healing to come with a prescription bottle and whispered judgments.

But responsibility, I learned, is also a form of self-love.

As human beings, we carry extraordinary healing potential within us. I believe that consciousness has the power to transform the body. There are individuals who, through profound awareness and regulation, have healed themselves and even others. Reaching that level of consciousness is something I aspire to.

But we are still living in this reality in bodies, in nervous systems shaped by trauma, environment, hormones, and stress, in a world that is not neutral to our biology. Healing at that level of consciousness is not easy, and pretending we are there when we are not can cause harm.

True prevention begins long before illness appears through regulation, nourishment, safety, and support. When a condition has already become chronic, returning to a healthy lifestyle is not optional; it is the first step, though not always the only one.

For me, understanding PMDD through neuroscience changed everything. The brain's sensitivity to allopregnanolone, a metabolite of progesterone, creates intense neurological activation during the luteal phase. Areas such as the prefrontal cortex experience overwhelming electrical activity. In that state, the brain is inflamed, overstimulated, and struggling to regulate itself. To deny support to the brain during that process is not strength; it is neglect.

Just as a person with insulin-dependent diabetes cannot simply decide to stop treatment and survive on intention alone, there are moments when the responsible choice is temporary, measured, and compassionate support.

Healing is not choosing sides: science or spirit, medication or mindfulness. It is choosing responsibility over self-punishment. It is meeting the brain where it is, not where we wish it would be. Choosing medical or therapeutic help without shame, without apology, and without asking permission, especially in a culture that pressures people to "push through," "heal naturally," or prove strength through suffering.

Every journey is different. No doctor knows your body better than you do. You are allowed to choose what feels aligned and safe for you, without shame, comparison, and spiritual bypassing.

Choosing Myself Was the Treatment

Spirituality entered as the next step. Instead of asking why this was happening to me, I began asking what my body was asking of me. That shift changed everything. Recognizing that something larger could hold me softened the isolation PMDD creates and reminded me that I was responding to years of unheld experience.

Energy work and family constellations revealed something my intellect had avoided: much of what I was carrying did not begin with me. Family Constellations, developed by Bert Hellinger, are based on the idea that families function as interconnected systems governed by hidden dynamics of belonging, order, and loyalty. According to Hellinger, unresolved trauma, exclusion, or imbalance in one generation can unconsciously influence the lives of those who come after, shaping emotional roles and patterns without conscious awareness. Central to this approach is the concept of the morphogenetic field, a theoretical field of information that holds the memory of a family system beyond individual experience. My body had inherited emotional roles long before I had language for them, such as caretaker, stabilizer, and container roles learned in childhood and reinforced through survival. Immigration only amplified them.

Family Constellations allowed me to step out of those roles, even briefly, and feel the relief of not holding everything anymore. My body responded immediately: less tension, more breath, a quiet permission to rest.

One of the most radical changes was learning to live in partnership with my cycle instead of against it. For years, I planned my life as if my body were static, as if energy and resilience were meant to be consistent every day of the month. PMDD shattered that illusion. Once I stopped fighting the reality of my cycle, I began organizing my life around it.

I learned when my energy naturally declined and stopped scheduling emotionally demanding tasks during those days. I learned when my nervous system needed more sleep, less stimulation, fewer conversations. I stopped apologizing for my body's needs, and this alone reduced the intensity of my symptoms.

The most transformative layer came when I began studying neuroscience. For the first time, my experiences made sense without moral judgment. I learned how trauma sensitizes the amygdala, how chronic stress disrupts the HPA axis, and how hormonal fluctuations interact with an already hypervigilant nervous system. PMDD was no longer a mystery or a flaw; it was a predictable response.

Understanding this removed shame.

Shame had been one of the most toxic contributors to my suffering, the belief that I was failing at being functional, failing at being stable, failing at being strong enough. Neuroscience reframed my experience as adaptive. My body had done exactly what it learned to do to survive.

That realization softened my internal dialogue. Instead of asking what was wrong with me, I began asking what my nervous system needed at that moment. Over time, PMDD changed form. The episodes became less catastrophic, less frightening. I no longer spiraled into panic about who I might become during those days. I learned to recognize early signals and intervene with care instead of fear.

Leadership began here as I took action on what I needed, slowed down based on self-respect, and listened to what my body needed. I no longer measure success by how much I can tolerate; I measure it by how well I can stay connected to myself when things get hard. I no longer see PMDD as an enemy to defeat, but as a signal that invites me back into alignment.

While resistance to regulation was not a straight line, it was a spiral one that brought me back to the same lessons at deeper levels, each time with more compassion, understanding, and agency.

My question to you is this: What would change if you asked what your body is asking for now and in the next hard moment, chose to listen, reaching for regulation rather than resistance?

Mapping the Unmapped

Navigating the Science and Soul of a Body in Flux

Robyn Straley

I did not expect the moment to feel the way it did.

I was sitting in a small exam room, hearing the diagnosis I had waited most of my life to receive, hypermobile Ehlers-Danlos. After fifty years of living in this body, someone had finally named the underlying architecture that shaped my joints, connective tissue, injuries, and the quirks I had carried since childhood. I thought having a name for it would bring clarity, or at least give me something solid to work with. I imagined a map, or at least a legend.

Instead, I heard, "Hypermobile Ehlers-Danlos Syndrome is a hereditary connective tissue disorder characterized by generalized joint hypermobility, tissue fragility, and multisystem involvement arising from dysregulation of collagen synthesis and extracellular matrix function."

Clear as mud.

In plain language, collagen is the scaffolding that holds your body together. It's the tensile web that supports ligaments and tendons, keeps joints aligned, gives skin its strength, and steadies and knits together the connective tissue from head to toe. With hypermobile Ehlers-Danlos, it isn't just a lack of collagen; it's the way the body assembles it. You can swallow all the supplements in the world, but your system will still break them down into raw materials and rebuild them in its own way, and that rebuilding process is where the blueprint falters.

The way I like to explain it to my neighbors here in the South is that my body appears to be purchasing its collagen at the Dollar General.

That basic truth matters. It means that the quality of the scaffolding is altered everywhere at once, in ways that are subtle until they are not. Things stretch a bit farther than expected. Joints move a bit more than they should. Injuries occur under loads that would be routine for other people. Healing is slower and less complete. What appears to be a scattered collection of minor problems is, in fact, one continuous pattern.

Uncharted Territory

Before any of this came sharply into focus, I had lived most of my life enjoying robust, uncomplicated health. I had an athlete's body that was strong, coordinated, and capable. My flexibility helped me in sports. Sure, I had longstanding quirks, including allergies, repeated ankle sprains, and joints that bent farther than other people's. But none of it felt like a "syndrome." It felt like my "normal" right up until midlife delivered a new map altogether, the kind whose topography forced me to reorient, recalibrate, and learn to navigate from scratch.

Perimenopause began around age forty-eight, and within a short time, my body changed in ways that startled me. One day, I ruptured a ligament in my ankle while simply walking. No dramatic story or fall, just a sudden, sharp, very painful injury.

My Iliotibial (IT) band tightened into a constant pull that led to trochanteric bursitis. Sleep became difficult because of hip and rib pain. My knees shifted slightly out of position and clicked back in with sharp discomfort. A rib began to slip and flare without warning. My thumbs became painful and unstable. My elbows developed tendon pain that refused to heal. My neck felt vulnerable in the mornings, and on more than one occasion, a single turn of my head triggered spasms severe enough that I could not move freely for days.

Daily life became negotiations with gravity. Hiking on uneven ground, which had always been one of my favorite things, became risky. Carrying groceries up the steep side steps to my house was no longer a simple task. Some days, I had to walk around to the front steps and take the gentler incline. I accumulated braces for various joints and rotated them depending on which part of my body needed reinforcement that day.

I kept telling myself that perimenopause was the only new factor and should therefore explain these changes. It did not. The symptoms involved multiple systems and arrived simultaneously. Joint instability, immune reactivity, migraines, gastrointestinal trouble, autonomic symptoms (a term that describes when the body's automatic regulation systems misfire), and sleep disruption all surfaced in the same season. There was no single, tidy explanation. Still, the lack of a tidy answer did not erase my need for one. I needed a way to make sense of the terrain to chart a path through an unfamiliar country.

My primary care doctor referred me to a rheumatologist, who did a full workup and eventually named what had been present since birth, hypermobile Ehlers-Danlos. The diagnosis connected many dots, yet it did not resolve the question that had begun circling in my mind. I understood that hypermobile Ehlers-Danlos involves low-quality collagen. I understood that perimenopause involved a natural reduction in collagen production. However, I wanted to know what happens when those two realities meet in one body.

That is how I ended up in another exam room.

A few months after my diagnosis, I sat in my gynecologist's office. He is widely regarded as a leader in his field, the kind of physician who trains other physicians. I arrived with a written list of the changes I could not ignore. I do not usually bring lists to appointments, but this time I needed the discipline of seeing everything in one place.

I asked the question that had been echoing in my mind. "What happens when someone with Ehlers-Danlos, a condition where the body builds collagen that is structurally weak, enters perimenopause, a stage of life when collagen production naturally declines? What happens when those forces meet?"

He read my list again and thought for a long moment. Then he said, with quiet honesty, "I don't know."

It felt as though the ground shifted underneath me. *If he did not know, who did? If no one knew, what did that mean for the path ahead?* I had assumed that somewhere, in some journal article or research university, this question had been answered.

The surprise was that there was no answer at all.

Yet something in me steadied. I realized I had been waiting for someone to accept the truth that no one had mapped this particular intersection: a body with fragile collagen entering a phase of life where collagen production declines. When my gynecologist said he did not know, he showed me the edge of the existing map.

The Edge of the Known World

I once saw a photograph of Etsy's headquarters. There was a sign on the wall that said, "We can do hard things." I think about that sign often. In that "I don't know" moment in the doctor's office, I made the decision to do a hard thing. I decided to claim my own healing process. If I wanted to move forward, I would have to begin mapping the next stretch myself.

That realization brought clarity and motivated me to search for answers. I tried a well-known functional medicine clinic and left with a lighter wallet and no clearer understanding. I visited patient forums and saw people who were understandably overwhelmed, trying many interventions at once, sometimes without medical guidance, and often shaping their entire identity around their condition. I had deep compassion for their pain, but I knew that approach was not right for me. I needed to remain grounded. I wanted to take my condition seriously without reducing it to nothing more than the sum of my symptoms.

When the intensity of symptoms began stacking on top of one another and altering my daily life, my only option in Western medicine was to enter the maze of specialists: rheumatology. hematology, immunology, urology, and gynecology. Each one peered at a single fragment of the whole, a narrow slice of the pie they'd been trained to interpret. But I was living in the overlap, in the blurry intersections where symptoms tangled and no single specialty claimed ownership.

Old school geographers used to create maps by stacking transparent sheets. One sheet shows elevation. Another shows rivers. Another shows vegetation. Another shows roads and towns. Each layer alone tells part of the story. When you stack them, patterns appear. You can see where rivers shape valleys, where towns cluster, and where land use changes.

Complex conditions behave the same way. My joint issues, immune issues, hormonal changes, autonomic symptoms, and neurological responses each represented one transparency. The specialists were not looking at the full stack, so I had to learn to see all the layers at once.

Once I accepted that the healthcare system would not assemble this map for me, my curiosity shifted. I began looking for researchers who were studying hypermobile Ehlers-Danlos with enough rigor to match the complexity of what I was living.

That search led me to the Norris Lab at the Medical University of South Carolina, which was conducting the first large-scale genetic study of hypermobile Ehlers-Danlos. The Norris Lab describes their work in a way that immediately resonated with me. They emphasize that patients are experts in complex diseases and that lived experience shapes the most meaningful scientific questions. Their patient-scientist initiative invites patients to participate as leaders in the research process rather than as subjects on the periphery. It affirmed something I have felt for a long time, which is that the perspective of the person living the condition is not a barrier to clarity but a source of direction and insight.

I asked my rheumatologist about participating in the research study. He reminded me that research data would be de-identified and that I would not receive personal results. He also pointed out that exploratory research rarely produces immediate clinical answers.

Determined, I explained that I was not looking for a cure. I wanted to leave the next breadcrumb on the trail for another traveler wandering through the same bewildering landscape. If I couldn't find my own way out yet, at least I could help illuminate the path for someone coming behind me.

I enrolled in the study, provided my DNA sample, completed the interviews, and waited. For years. Every so often, I would check to see whether a paper had been released. Each time, there was nothing. I reminded myself that meaningful science takes time, and research timelines rarely match the pace that an impatient patient would prefer.

Eventually, the paper appeared.

Discovering a New Landscape

Reading it felt like watching fog lift off a landscape I already knew by heart. The study confirmed that hypermobile Ehlers-Danlos is not caused by a single broken gene. Instead, it arises from multiple subtle genetic variations that alter how systems communicate. The strongest associations were not in collagen genes. They were in regulatory regions that influence signaling in the nervous system, immune system, autonomic functions, and pain pathways.

In other words, your body is sending group texts where no one reads the full thread. Systems are doing things without talking to one another. Signals are scrambled in unhelpful ways.

For the first time, a scientific map resembled the lived experience of patients like me. I was one of the more than eighteen hundred participants whose DNA helped to draw that map. That mattered to me and added a lantern to a path I had once walked in the dark.

After reading the paper, I met with a genetic counselor to explore testing that could connect my individual genome to the new research.

She was thoughtful and direct. Clinical labs can test for Ehlers-Danlos types caused by known single-gene mutations. Those are the subtypes with catastrophic changes to one gene. Hypermobile Ehlers-Danlos does not have a single-gene cause, so it is not eligible for those panels. A connective tissue panel could rule out types I already knew I did not have. It could not confirm the type I did have.

She recommended that I check again in a year or two, in case clinical protocols evolve. She was doing her job correctly. The system was doing what it was designed to do. Unfortunately, what it was designed to do did not yet include autonomy, agency, or voice for the patient. The system had no way to support questions that fell outside its predefined boxes, even with a scientific paper to back the play.

As I embraced the next step in my journey, I realized the system could not follow me. I would have to go around. I want to map my own genome onto the findings from the study. I want to know where I fall within the coordinates the researchers described. If I am going to be the cartographer of my own healing, I want to work with the most accurate map available. This means that I will be paying out of pocket for high-resolution whole-genome sequencing through a commercial lab that works directly with patients.

Tracing the Blueprint

Whole-genome sequencing will not give me a cure or a treatment plan, but it will deepen my understanding. Seeing the whole landscape helps me make thoughtful, coordinated decisions, communicate more effectively with clinicians, and move forward intentionally rather than reactively. That orientation toward understanding is simply how I now live and heal.

The study told a clear story about how hypermobile Ehlers-Danlos behaves across systems, and I already know, at a gut level, that I match that landscape. Having precise genetic information will help me approach my next medical appointment with clarity, grounding, and precise language. It would allow me to say, "Here is the scientific paper, here are my results, and here is the pattern they create." It changes the conversation and shifts the dynamic from guesswork to informed collaboration.

My next step is to choose the right clinic. I will do my research, choose a clinic that feels right, and then wait. Waiting is a familiar part of the complex condition landscape, and long waiting lists for new patient appointments are a familiar part of this terrain.

When the appointment arrives, I will walk in with my data in hand. I want the conversation to begin from a place where they see me as a whole person.

I am still in midjourney, but here is what I know for sure: We must listen closely to our own bodies and learn to distinguish the signal from the noise. Patterns matter more than isolated events. Making five changes at once might feel productive, but it makes it impossible to trace cause and effect. The scientific mindset is surprisingly simple: Choose one hypothesis, consult with your physician, make one change, observe carefully, and then decide what to try next.

Throughout this journey, I have also learned that we need to build our own medical teams that embrace curiosity. One test I use is to bring a scientific paper to an appointment, and I watch what happens. If the doctor takes the paper, reads it with interest, asks questions, and is willing to learn alongside me, that person is usually one of my companions. If they dismiss it, they aren't a good fit for me.

Complex patients have to hold their own map. Clinicians walk alongside us for stretches of the trail. Good ones make a meaningful difference. The continuity, however, belongs to us.

If you are standing at your own trailhead, unsure what comes next, there are a few things I hope you carry with you:

You can begin from uncertainty.

You can gather your tools.

You can do hard things.

You can learn to understand science, one concept at a time.

You can remember that you are more than your diagnosis.

Start with a pause and look honestly at the landscape ahead. Then you begin, step by step, with a lantern held just high enough to see the next few feet of the path.

It's been years since my diagnosis, and I have not found every answer or walked out of the maze. Instead, I have learned to work with what is in front of me and know that healing is not a straight line. It is iterative and often slow. It is grounded in curiosity, clarity, and a willingness to keep going even when the route is unmarked.

Viktor Frankl wrote that when we are no longer able to change a situation, we are challenged to change ourselves. That line has stayed with me. It speaks to the core of complex healing. The terrain may be unfamiliar, and we may hold an incomplete map. We still have choices about how we walk. We can change the way we pay attention and respond to uncertainty. We can change the way we carry our own story.

Skin to the Soul

THE LONG WAY HOME TO MY BODY

Jena Burton

My story doesn't start with childhood trauma or a dramatic health crisis.

Have you ever felt insecure because of your skin issues? You leave the house, and it feels like that's all everyone sees. This is how I felt, and it was the commencement of my healing journey. If you've ever dealt with inflammatory skin issues, especially on your face, you know how deeply it can affect your confidence and how you show up in the world. What confused me most was that I had never struggled with acne as a teenager. Suddenly, in my early twenties, rash-like breakouts appeared out of nowhere. I couldn't understand why.

Looking back, the reason feels obvious. At the time, I simply didn't have the language, tools, or understanding to connect the dots. That confusion was the first nudge toward a path that would ultimately change my life.

In 2011, I was working my first job out of college at a designer consignment store in Chicago. Fashion had always been my dream, and between that job and my fashion blog gaining traction, I felt excited about my early career. On the surface, everything looked good. At the same time, I began experiencing anxiety for the first time in my life. I had always been a worrier—the responsible one—but I had never felt anxiety in my body. It took a long time to recognize what I was experiencing. I knew people who said they "had anxiety," but I didn't truly understand what that meant until I was living it.

I felt extreme nervousness every morning as I walked through those doors, with knots in my stomach, nausea, and a growing list of digestive issues. I chalked it up to having a sensitive stomach, something I'd been told I had since childhood after being born with acid reflux. Looking back now, with everything I've learned, I can see how early my body learned to live in a state of vigilance. I wouldn't be surprised if I came into this world with a dysregulated nervous system, shaped by a stressful birth and reinforced by years of feeling unsafe without knowing why.

The office drama I experienced became the spark that brought the anxiety to the surface. I ignored it, mostly because I didn't yet understand it. Instead, I focused on fixing what I could see, my skin. I bounced between dermatologists, estheticians, and allergists, trying anything that promised relief. Nothing worked. In fact, harsh topical treatments often made things worse. I felt determined but exhausted, certain something deeper was happening internally, yet unsure how to uncover it.

Many of us have gone through a similar pattern, where we're dealing with a chronic symptom, or multiple symptoms, and we're doing "all of the right things," yet everything leads to a dead end. We feel defeated and hopeless. That's how I felt. I know what it's like firsthand to feel ashamed of symptoms while simultaneously hitting that brick wall of frustration.

Five years later, I was introduced to functional medicine, and everything shifted.

When My Body Finally Had a Voice

For the first time, a practitioner sat with me for over an hour and asked questions no one had ever asked before.

"How long had I been on hormonal birth control? What were my stress levels like? How did I manage stress?"

I remember thinking, *What does any of this have to do with acne?*

Testing revealed severe gut dysbiosis—too little beneficial bacteria and far too much harmful bacteria. My doctor explained the gut-skin connection and how the gut influences every system in the body. I suddenly understood my body in a completely new way. A door opened that I didn't even know existed.

At the time, my lifestyle looked a little something like going to events five nights a week, drinking champagne, eating at restaurants or catered food, staying up too late, never feeling well-rested, rarely cooking at home, and not exercising. I can't complain, though, as I had a lot of fun in my twenties, and I don't regret any of it. Life's challenges present themselves as an opportunity for us to grow.

Healing took nearly a year. I changed how I ate, prioritizing protein and cooked vegetables. I had to start focusing on foods that were easy to digest. This can be counterintuitive for those who think salads are healthy, for example. Yes, they are (I used to eat a lot of them!) But if you have gut issues, raw vegetables are difficult to break down and can cause more GI upset. This is one of those examples of feeling like you're doing the "right" thing and it backfires. With this diet change, along with cycling through various supplements prescribed by my functional medicine doctor, I got to a place where I could reintroduce foods. I felt like I was in a good place. At the time, I believed I was healed. In reality, I had only just begun.

Around that same period, chronic neck pain crept in and stayed. I tried physical therapy, acupuncture, massage, and chiropractic care. Each offered temporary relief, but the pain always returned. Practitioners were surprised by the level of tension in my body at such a young age. I felt frustrated and defeated, unaware that my nervous system was quietly holding everything I hadn't yet learned how to process.While I was no longer in that toxic work environment, I still felt the effects. I was also in a relationship that my parents did not support, and I was carrying over two decades of not feeling safe in my body. I remember the news being on in my house growing up, and although my parents had the best intentions to protect me, I always felt like the world was a scary place. Over time, that feeling manifested into neck pain, acne, and even chronic bladder infections as a child. This sense of safety, or lack thereof, has felt ingrained in me on a cellular level.

Even after my gut improved, the anxiety remained. I was doing everything I thought I should, such as eating clean and exercising, but I wasn't caring for my mind. Eventually, I began cognitive behavioral therapy. I hesitated at first, convinced my worries about the state of the world were normal. I imagined I couldn't be the only one fearful of public places, thinking anyone could open fire at any moment. Between the mass shootings nationally and the crime in Chicago, where I lived, the lack of safety I felt both internally and externally was something I could no longer handle on my own. This is why I entered therapy, but what I left with was far more than I could have imagined.

Before therapy, I rarely cried. I lived in a muted emotional state—neither truly happy nor deeply sad. I was guarded, judgmental, and disconnected from my own vulnerability. During one session, my therapist guided me through a loving-kindness meditation. I didn't know what to expect, but something shifted almost immediately. As I was asked to direct compassion toward myself, then toward others—people I loved, people I barely knew, and even those I found difficult—I felt something inside me soften.

It was the first time I realized how little grace I had given myself, and how tightly I had been holding the world at arm's length. That moment cracked me open, and it became a turning point in my healing, teaching me that compassion, especially self-compassion, was the doorway to feeling safe, connected, and human again.

Over time, that protective shell fell away as I developed empathy, compassion, and emotional range. For the first time, I felt both the highs and the lows. This was where the real healing began.

The Pause That Changed Everything

When the world shut down in 2020, my healing paused again. Like so many others, I was forced inward. During that time, I discovered Melissa Wood Health, a gentler form of movement that reshaped my relationship with exercise. For years, I believed workouts had to be punishing to be effective. This slower, more intentional movement taught me that exercise could be nourishment rather than discipline. Through this more connected way of moving my body, I began strengthening my relationship with myself, a theme that would later become the foundation of my work.

Meditation found me slowly. I resisted it for years, convinced my racing mind wasn't built for stillness. It took experimentation and reframing to understand that meditation wasn't about stopping thoughts but observing them without judgment. When my husband and I bought our home in 2021, I committed to daily practice. There was something about this new start that made me feel more motivated to commit, a similar feeling to why we commit to resolutions in the new year. It's a fresh start.

Meditation brought clarity, patience, and peace. With that clarity came a realization: The marketing work I did was no longer aligned. I had spent nearly a decade on my healing journey and felt pulled toward wellness, but I lacked credentials. Then, one day, an email from mindbodygreen landed in my inbox announcing their health coaching program. It felt like a missing puzzle piece.

I enrolled in the program in late summer of 2023. A few months later, I found out I was pregnant. My plan to juggle marketing and coaching fell apart as my marketing clients disappeared. I took it as a sign to fully commit. At six months pregnant, I earned my National Board certification, an achievement I remain incredibly proud of.

When Everything Fell Apart

Soon after, grief entered my life in a way I had never known. My deaf white boxer, Lennox, suddenly lost the use of his back legs. Watching his fear broke my heart. Choosing the gift of rest, as my vet would say, was the hardest decision I had ever made. The grief was consuming. I couldn't eat, meditate, or function. I cried and survived moment by moment.

Weeks after giving birth, while my newborn son spent three days in the NICU, my other dog, Laz, declined rapidly. I came home from the hospital to say goodbye again. Grieving two beloved companions while recovering from childbirth and learning how to care for a newborn was the most challenging season of my life. The combination of sleep deprivation, raging hormones, immense grief, missing my dogs so intensely, not being able to breastfeed despite my efforts, and recovering from the most mentally and physically demanding event of my life.

It was unlike anything I've ever experienced. Like the walls came crashing down at once. When I think back on that time today, I'm amazed I got through it all.

I survived because of the tools I had built over years of healing, although they looked different during this intense time. For example, I was not able to meditate. This was a hard pill for me to swallow. I depended on meditation for my mental health and strength. I tried many times, but all I could do was cry uncontrollably. Though I wasn't able to meditate, I could still practice mindfulness and take the lessons I've learned from my practice.

Instead, I practiced grace, like how I learned from the loving-kindness meditation. I didn't need to do the meditation to remember the feeling I got from it. We are all out here doing our best, even if we don't always see it in ourselves and others. I reminded myself that pain is temporary, both the physical and emotional pain. Some days, brushing my teeth was a victory. When I was able to regain a little strength and walk around the block, I felt even just one percent better. Eating a nourishing meal, I was grateful I prepped and froze while pregnant, was a huge win. Those reframes saved me.

In 2025, I finally healed my chronic pain through nervous system work. For the first time in over a decade, my body felt safe. I learned that healing isn't about fixing ourselves. It's about learning how to listen.

Everything I lived through led me into service, leadership, and deep devotion to myself.

Coming Home to Myself

Healing didn't come from one protocol or breakthrough moment. It came from building safety within myself, again and again.

The practice I now live by and guide others through is devotion to self-connection. This begins by listening to the body rather than overriding it.

I ask, *What do I need right now to feel even slightly safer?*

Some days, that looks like journaling or meditation. Other days, it means rest, nourishment, or allowing grief to move through me.

When anxiety, pain, or exhaustion arises, I redefine success. Small acts of care matter. Over time, these moments rebuild trust within the body. Cooking yourself a nourishing meal, listening to an inspirational podcast, taking a walk outside, letting it all out in your journal, dancing to your favorite song—these are all ways of telling your body *I see you, I hear you, I care about you.*

Instead of asking what's wrong with me, I ask what I'm protecting myself from. Is it judgment? Shame? Guilt? Fear?

I've always naturally gone to the worst-case scenario. Now I know two things: 1) the chance of that scenario is *highly* unlikely, and 2) if it does happen, I am equipped to handle it. That shift alone transformed my relationship with my body.

Healing is about strengthening the relationship with ourselves so we can hold both joy and grief. From that place, leadership becomes embodied, compassionate, and sustainable. We all carry innate joy, love, and peace within us. We are born with it. As we move through life, layers of limiting beliefs form shaped by caregivers, peers, teachers, and society. Healing gently peels those layers back, guiding us home to who we truly are beneath the conditioning.

This understanding has transformed how I show up as both a mother and a coach. I'm able to see people for who they are at their core, even when they can't see it themselves. I lead with presence instead of fixing, curiosity instead of judgment, and compassion instead of urgency. I trust that healing unfolds when people feel safe, supported, and deeply seen. It's from this place that I now live, parent, and serve, rooted in hope, grounded in self-trust, and devoted to helping others reconnect with the wholeness that has always been within them.

Hot Girls Club

Finding Confidence and Sisterhood in the Dojo

Raven Petty

"Breathe in through your nose and out through your mouth," Sensei instructed us. "Slow down, walk around, and just breathe."

With my face beet red and sweat pouring from my head, I simply nodded. It was the only gesture I could make after thirty minutes of punching, kicking, and dodging, trying not to get hit by my partner.

Then I gave Sensei a big smile, mouth guard showing and all, to let her know I was okay and having fun.

This happens almost every Thursday night in karate class. We warm up, practice correct form, then pair off to score points using what we've learned. Bounce, duck, punch, dodge, jump back, bounce, kick, block, counter, jump back, and the dance goes on. Sometimes my *kumite* (sparring) partner is a good girlfriend, sometimes it's a guy twice my size, and other times it's a teen who can bounce circles around me. Regardless of the partner, the goal is to score without hurting the other person. Class is not the place to cause injury. Instead, we're here to bring out the best in each other.

Barely Breathing

A few years ago, the ability to do cardio, much less maintain sport-style combat for a half-hour, was not on the table. First of all, I was out of shape, not overweight, just not healthy enough to exercise. I had spent twenty-plus years at a desk and smoked cigarettes. Most weeks focused on work, leaving little time for anything but survival.

Over the years, I became short of breath and not motivated to exercise. While I enjoyed yoga and water activities, daily exercise was a big, "hell no." The idea of joining a gym or running outside in Nashville's four-season climate did not appeal to me. Exercise also felt inconvenient in my wake-up, work, sleep, repeat routine. Aside from not being interested, there was the added judgment I placed on myself and the picture-perfect wellness coaches who flooded my social media feeds.

When you huff and puff and compare your body to others, it doesn't leave much room for taking risks or trying new things.

The Quest Begins

Some say when you hit a certain age, you begin to question life. If there is such a thing as a midlife re-invention, I jumped in feet first when life started to feel too predictable, boring, and not what I wanted.

One of the many things that changed was that I quit smoking, which served as a catalyst for a new career and a newfound desire to move my body. However, health experts recommend waiting six weeks to exercise after quitting due to the strain on your heart and lungs. When it was safe to begin, I tried online challenges, explored hiking trails, and walked. I spent a few years trying new things like ziplining, white-water rafting, rage rooms, and kayaking, hoping to find something that

I could stick with long-term. While these activities were full of memories and hi-jinks, regular exercise still felt like a chore.

As a coach, I see it all the time. We start something new <insert yoga, dance, themed gyms, meditation, writing, painting, more protein, etc.>, and as soon as the newness wears off, we find reasons why we can't do it. Out of nowhere come late nights at the office, car trouble, something with the kids, or a cold, so we miss a class. Then one turns into two, and the next thing we know, we wonder why we're bored and out of shape while sitting on the couch binge-watching a show.

What we don't realize is that we need a combination of things to succeed. When we begin a new habit, we need a supportive environment, time in our calendar, and the motivation to stay consistent. Everything in our lives must support this new habit. And that's much easier said than done.

When I made these changes in my mid-thirties, I had the best guy friends, a son, husband, two brothers, and a boy dog. This girl was surrounded by men all the time, and as we know, too much of something isn't a good thing. Nonetheless, I was a guy's girl, something that developed from early adolescence because hanging out with men was more comfortable, fun, and easy. Even today, some of my best friends are men I've known for decades.

Now in the trenches of a midlife reinvention, I found myself feeling alone with no one to talk to about all the things women experience, like body changes, wellness goals, romcoms, clothes, jewelry, sex, marriage, motherhood, books, and the list goes on. When something happened, and I wanted a friend, there was something, or someone, missing.

Please understand that I did have amazing colleagues and confidants who were women. We had good relationships that felt more mom-like because they were at least ten, some twenty years older. While these women provided guidance and companionship, some topics were off the table. Plus, each had their own family, stress, career, and goals, so consistent communication was rare. My heart craved women around my own age with whom I could feel accepted and free.

Using my analytical brain, I went into research mode. While I didn't search for "how to make women friends," I started by reading only books written by women. There's no better way to learn about women than reading their stories. Then I baby-stepped my way into social events, a leap for this textbook introvert. I contacted former colleagues for lunch and signed up for book clubs. Then I hosted webinars and created social media pages, hoping to build a community of like-minded women.

After several years and all of this effort, I found myself in my forties with the best guy friends, a son, husband, two brothers, and a boy dog.

Despite all of the connections, there still wasn't a woman around my age who I could call during a tough day or just someone to girl-talk with. Social pages stopped getting engagement. Some women even felt the need to compete or gossip about me. Women know when other women talk behind their backs, and while I always try to take the high road, some relationships aren't meant to be.

Same shit, different day vibes hit hard. Now I not only felt alone, but frustrated from all of the rejection. Depression moved in as my mental health took a toll, and I started asking questions like, "What's wrong with me?" "Why don't women like me?" "Am I weird?" "How can I be more like other women, so they will accept me?"

This spiral went on as I invited my friends, bourbon, ice cream, and reruns to the pity party. None of these questions were on-brand for this Aquarian, who has no trouble being the "no-BS, this is what you get" kinda girl. The rejection from others had cut so deeply that some days I would sob with the belief that I was always going to feel alone and different. I sat in this rejection mindset for a while, venting to all of the men in my life about not having any girl friends. Bless them. They did try to understand and provided space for me, and I'm forever grateful to them.

On the flip side, I've done enough personal development work to know these things weren't true. The truth was, however, I still felt alone and hopeless that I would never find true friendship with other women. Even a desperate "how to make women friends" search yielded everything I had already tried. Now what was I supposed to do?

Enter the Dragon

Martial arts were never on my bucket list. A few friends and family have spent some time competing, so karate wasn't a completely foreign concept, but my decision to sign up shocked some people.

I'm sure many people thought it was part of my mid-life ~~crisis~~ reinvention because what introverted forty-something book-nerd decides to jump into a martial art with no experience? To those who know me, it probably seemed like something random I would likely quit.

But I was so bored. At night, my body screamed through restless legs, and months of slight weight gain started to impact how I looked at myself in the mirror. I needed something challenging and different, so I called two karate studios in the area. Only one called me back, and I knew within five minutes of talking with her that I had made the right decision. The woman's voice was friendly and firm, no-nonsense, which I can relate to.

The introductory offer was simple: Free uniform and four classes for twenty-five bucks.

As of 2026, that was two years ago.

The first few classes were full of anxiety and confusion as my body learned to move differently. And boy, did I sweat. We're talking full detox sweats that made my hair frizz and cheeks flush. With Sensei's guidance and never-ending patience, over time, I learned to move with more confidence. The depression fog lifted each time I went to class and watched Sensei correct our forms and give pep-talks, knowing that she had our best interests at heart. In karate, you can't fake it. How you show up is what you get from it. Even today, as I write this, a smile stretches across my face thinking of her firm but kind fierceness that keeps us in line.

At the same time, something else magical was happening.

Other adults at the dojo welcomed me with open arms. Classmates, aged fifteen to sixty, and I would stand in small groups chatting, practicing, and laughing. All walks of life and backgrounds came together and genuinely supported one another—not just in karate but through life struggles and celebrating the wins. This is what a community should do.

Little did I know that some of these classmates would become the women friends that this guy's girl had always hoped for.

Welcome to the Club

A few months into training, there was a group of women who talked me into a competition. Meet the Hot Girls Club. Not only are these women beautiful, fit, and strong—in all ages, sizes, and shapes—they draw others into a world full of diversity. We're talking different nationalities, cultures, ballet, heavy metal, body-building, bowlers, artists, executives, military veterans, and boss-girl energy. Many are moms, all of them are there to become better versions of themselves. Plus, any one of them knows exactly where to punch to make someone hit the ground.

The first competition occurred a few months after my first class. Did I win? Absolutely not. Was I scared? Absolutely not.

The women in my class prepared me. We walked through the stages of competition, what judges score, and what they expected me to know. During the competition, they cheered for me and offered tips. While I felt some butterflies, I enjoyed watching others compete, their seamless way of flipping the switch from their daily self to an intimidating goddess with fists of fury. The women in our class are terrifying in the best way.

That competition was the first time I felt accepted by other women for exactly as I am—a strong-willed, opinionated, curious leader who loves to up my game. While there are many things that make us different from one another, we have qualities that draw us to each other. We're intelligent, hard-working, enjoy learning, determined, have a sense of humility, offer compassion, prioritize wellness, and we're all super hot because we embrace our strength, beauty, and bodies. And we tell each other these things. Any given class is packed full of compliments, love, and encouragement.

As I got to know and spar with these women, our friendships grew deeper. Classes led to birthday brunches, concerts, game days, and even helping each other move. At annual picnics and holiday parties, you'll find us laughing and sharing plates, then helping clean up. When we go out, we encourage each other to flaunt what we've got. We've built long-lasting relationships of sisterhood founded on mutual respect. Every woman in our dojo is a member of the Hot Girls Club.

The best part? The competition stays in the dojo where it belongs.

Each woman I've met practicing karate has helped me build confidence, not only in the dojo but in all aspects of life. Getting to know them has helped me become more comfortable around women and embrace newcomers with the same enthusiasm that encouraged me on day one.

At home, I speak up for what I need. As a coach, I speak with authority as I lead others in completing their books. My head lifts higher as I enter rooms with powerful entrepreneurs and people who make a difference in their respective communities. At events, I dress to impress. What karate demands of my mind and body, paired with the community, helped me realize I am astonishing and want to exude that energy inside and out. If I can feel attractive while dripping in sweat and wearing a mouth guard, I can certainly work a networking event.

Our energy calls in more of what we want, and I want gorgeous, fierce women secure in who they are and what they want in life. Sometimes it takes bold action and an open heart. Sometimes it takes labored breathing and sore muscles. Sometimes a step out of our comfort zone isn't enough; we have to leap and follow our gut instinct.

Nearly two years in, I've stopped trying to fit into traditional boxes of womanhood. Instead, I fight for my place among the fierce. My breath is no longer labored by smoke or survival. Today, my breath is fueled by the confidence of a woman who knows she can take a hit, glove-tap, laugh, and go to lunch afterwards. That freedom is the ultimate breath of fresh air.

Anatomy of the Loop

The final mirror before the soulmate

Lucianna Genova

What happens when the human mind mistakes familiarity for truth? It is a cycle where the same emotional trigger leads to the same choices, which create the same results over and over again until something interrupts it. What if loops are not repetition but dressed as destiny?

Dopamine is often mistaken for the chemical of pleasure, but more accurately it's the chemical of *pursuit*. Dopamine does not care about satisfaction. It cares about movement toward something, wanting, imagining, hoping. Dopamine lives in the space of *almost*. Before the kiss. Before the answer. Before the ending.

I did not know these words for most of my life.
I only knew the feeling.

Sitting and watching the film *Elena Undone* was what unsettled me first. I could feel dopamine wake up in my body before I understood why. The familiar rush moved through me before my thoughts could catch up. The excitement of secrecy, the pull of closed doors, the heightened electricity of watching the chase unfold, and the quiet hope that somehow it would all resolve into a happily ever after. I recognized it immediately.

When it came to romantic relationships, my brain had never asked whether something was sustainable. It asked whether it felt alive. My chest would tighten, my breath shorter, something inside me leaned forward in anticipation.

I wasn't chasing unavailable people because I wanted pain. I wasn't avoiding real love. I was chasing intensity.

Naming the Loop

Over the years, I didn't know I was looping. That is the nature of loops. They feel like fate, arriving with good timing and a mischievous grin.

I told myself I was drawn to depth, intensity, and women who stirred something ancient and electric in me. I believed I loved fiercely, unapologetically, with a heart too large for simple love stories. That explanation followed me for years, and I wore it like a badge of honor.

What I didn't know, and what no one ever explained, was that the brain can mistake familiarity for truth. Inside my body, familiarity felt like recognition, and recognition felt like destiny, which gave me meaning.

The cruel trick is that while you're inside a loop, it doesn't feel repetitive. Each story feels different. Each beginning carries the promise that *this time* might be the one. The endings, however, always arrive wearing the same face.

Unavailable women came in many forms. Some were married. Others were straight. Some lived in-between. We would share late nights, hidden conversations, stolen moments that felt cinematic, dangerous, and intensely alive.

There was always a reason it couldn't be simple, and somehow, I mistook that difficulty for depth.

What I see now is that I wasn't addicted to the women themselves. I was addicted to anticipation.

Neuroscience has a word for this called dopamine.

Dopamine lived in my body like a whisper. My brain, loyal, intelligent, and doing exactly what it had been trained to do, kept choosing scenarios where resolution was impossible. Unavailable people do not demand endings. Instead, they offer fantasy. The rush would arrive before the kiss, not after it. In the ache of *what if.* It did not care how the story ended. It only cared that the chase continued. It was chemistry speaking louder than reason. And I followed the voice that had been trained the longest.

When Familiar Felt Like Love

Along the way, I hurt good people. Women who were kind, open, emotionally available and willing to build something real. They didn't ignite my nervous system, and I told myself the connection wasn't right. Sometimes I walked away abruptly, sometimes gently.

Looking back, I can tell the truth without cruelty that my brain wasn't being fed the chemistry it had learned to crave.

Good love felt quiet and that felt suspicious.

Chaos, on the other hand, felt familiar.

Familiarity is not the same as safety, but the nervous system doesn't know that at first. Our systems don't ask whether something is good for us but asks whether it is known. What we experience repeatedly, especially early on, becomes the baseline our body recognizes as normal.

This is how chaos earns its power.

There was another layer beneath all of this, one I didn't recognize for a long time because it had been disguised as success. I grew up swimming competitively. In that world, love had rules.

For example, when I won, I was rewarded with praise, attention, approval, and relief. When I performed well, I was seen, valued, and safe. Dopamine arrived with applause, so relief settled into my muscles like permission to exhale.

When I lost, the atmosphere in my household changed. Silence followed while shame entered the room. Anger lingered. Consequences landed not just on my body, but on my sense of worth. During those times, cortisol took over then, tightening everything, reminding me to stay alert.

My nervous system learned this early and learned it well that love followed performance. Over time, my body learned that connection was something you earned under pressure, not something freely given. Intensity became meaningful. Effort turned into intimacy. Ease felt undeserved.

When love is conditional early on, the nervous system adapts by staying vigilant. It learns that rest is temporary and safety must be maintained through pursuit. It felt like responsibility.

Quiet love, however, registered as the calm before punishment, so my brain did what it knew how to do. It chose relationships that kept me activated, chasing, hoping, proving, enduring, because that state felt like love. It was familiar. I didn't consciously create this pattern. It was formed long before I knew how to question it, but understanding it became my responsibility.

The Mirror That Didn't Look Away

Then came the relationship that brought the pattern into my home, where there was nowhere left to perform or hide. Since I began caring for my mother, no partner had lived in this house with me.

Lena would be the first. She was a yoga instructor who lived in Naples. On the surface, she felt calm in a way I trusted, intentional, well-practiced, and fluent in the language of healing. Being around her slowed me down, or at least made me believe I was slowing down.

She told me she was in the process of ending a marriage, but the whole story came in pieces. Always partial and unresolved. Her husband existed more as an outline than a person. There was just enough truth to believe her and just enough distance to keep me hoping.

Looking back, I understand now that my loop didn't end because I found someone good. It ended because the cost of staying in the pattern finally exceeded what my body was getting from it. However, that moment didn't arrive when I got hurt. I had learned how to tolerate that. The turning point arrived when I realized my choices were destabilizing someone I am wired to protect.

My mother was born with cerebral palsy and is disabled. When my grandmother passed in 2013, the responsibility of her care shifted into my hands. I live with my mother in the home she chose to remain in for the rest of her life. I hold the rhythm of a life that cannot be rushed or destabilized.

When the chaos of that romantic relationship entered my home, I felt something rupture inside me. The pattern was no longer contained within my own body. Now it was touching the one place I had vowed to keep safe. That realization crossed a line in my nervous system I could not uncross. A simple and devastating realization, my choices were no longer just hurting me; they were hurting someone who loved me. Dopamine fell silent then because it no longer had permission to run free. This wasn't guilt. It was a new identity.

When Lena moved into my home, everything changed. Fantasy requires distance, surviving on absence and projection. Living together removed all of it. Reality entered the room every day, and once it did, I could no longer edit the story.

The red flags were loud. The lies stopped being spiritualized. When the betrayal came, it landed with a finality I had never felt before. She did not hurt my mother. Not directly, verbally, or physically. The shift happened as my mother watched *me be hurt.* My mother saw the quiet unraveling and confusion, the grief I tried to carry without letting it spill into the room. Something inside me stopped.

I had learned how to tolerate pain aimed at myself. I had learned how to explain it away, minimize it, and survive it. Watching my mother witness that pain, and watching her carry concern she couldn't fix, crossed a line I didn't know existed.

It had always been okay to hurt me. It was not okay to let her watch it happen.

For the first time, I saw the loop from beginning to end, not just the intoxicating middle.

I remember saying the words out loud, "I'm so sick of my own self." I didn't mean it with cruelty but felt clarity. It wasn't shameful; it was a recalibration.

Once that truth settled into my body, the behavior stopped feeling tempting. We felt incompatible. It wasn't dramatic. There was no vow, declaration, or moment of triumph. It was quiet and felt like something ancient in me standing up and saying, "Enough."

For years, my nervous system had learned how to survive instability by knowing how to track moods, read subtext, and anticipate shifts. It knew how to stay awake inside love, how to brace for impact, how to remain useful even while being hurt. It had also kept me looping.

Caring for my mother requires a different kind of strength because there is no performance in it.

Somewhere along the way, caring for her taught me something my old relationships never had: empathy is a practice. I learned to put myself in other people's shoes, not as an idea, but as a daily question.

If this were me, what would I want?

That question guides how I move through the world, but it matters most with her. It isn't always easy, and I don't always do it perfectly. I make mistakes, but I know what it feels like to be overlooked, reduced to a limitation instead of seen as a whole person. I want her to live the rest of her life feeling expanded in her creativity, dignity, and freedom.

There is no exciting reward in that kind of love. There is only integrity, and for the first time, my body recognized that as enough. No applause. No reward chemistry at the end of the day. There is only responsibility, presence, and follow-through. Love, stripped of drama. Love that does not spike or crash. Love that simply continues. I had spent years mistaking activation for aliveness. But this steady devotion, this quiet endurance, was aliveness too. Dopamine had trained me to reach forward. Caregiving taught me how to stay.

Over time, I began to understand that the part of me drawn to intensity wasn't broken. It was overworked because it had carried the responsibility of connection for too long. Once it was allowed to rest, it stopped demanding chaos as proof of love. I haven't rejected my past, but because I outgrew the chemistry that once governed it. What had once felt magnetic now felt misaligned. What had once felt irresistible now felt exhausting.

The Choice That Changed the Pattern

There is a moment after a loop breaks when nothing rushes in to replace it. The only thing left is just space. At first, that felt uncomfortable. My nervous system kept scanning for something to chase. Dopamine hovered, waiting for instruction, but nothing came. That was the point.

For the first time in my adult life, I wasn't choosing from hunger or negotiating my worth inside someone else's uncertainty. I had seen the loop clearly now, not as a moral failure, but as a lived pattern. And once a pattern is seen end to end, it loses its spell. Intensity no longer masqueraded as intimacy. Activation was no longer disguised itself as connection. Chemistry, I understood now, was not the same as compatibility. While these sensations themselves were never mistakes, they are part of how connection begins.

When love arrived without obstacles in a new relationship, my body didn't immediately recognize it. There was presence, consistency, and availability. At first, my old instincts whispered questions. *Is this too easy? Why does my body feel unfamiliar inside something so steady?* But this time, I stayed in this unfamiliar space.

Staying changed everything.

Other chemicals began to speak then, oxytocin and serotonin, like soft voices I had never learned to listen for. As they emerged, they began to build. This new love, now my wife, didn't rescue me from this work. With resolve, she reflected back to me and showed me that the steadiness I once mistook for quiet was alignment. She mirrored the life I was already living, protective and devoted, and grounded, was not something to escape, but something to honor.

The loop had ended because I became incompatible with chaos and let these other things live within me. I don't regret the woman I was before I understood this. She was doing the best she could with the chemistry and conditioning she had been given. But I don't live from that place anymore. Now, when intensity appears, I pause. When mystery feels magnetic, I ask what it's protecting. When chaos dresses itself up as destiny, I recognize the costume.

Love no longer needs to hurt to feel meaningful. Love doesn't need to be earned or chased. Now I choose love consciously, consistently, and with presence.

That is the anatomy of the loop.

I didn't lose passion. I gained depth.

I didn't stop feeling. I took off the armor I'd learned to wear around love.

I didn't settle. I returned home to my truest self.

I didn't dull love. I deepened it.

This is how it ends.

Rising with Clarity

Untethering from Old Stories to Own Your Truth

Maria Barrett

I'm stepping out of perfectionism to say, "Hell, YES!" to you and me! Stepping way out of my comfort zone and into my natural badass, authentic self. Letting my highest intention guide me to help me not abandon or betray myself and my highest intention. I realize it is generous to share my stories to help others feel seen and not alone, and it gives me the opportunity to see what's possible.

I don't say any of these stories lightly, or to stay in the emotion of them. It is to give some insight and truth, and what led me back home to me.

The Weight of Being Unseen

I was told, by multiple extended family members, that my mother never wanted me. I felt it, all my life, in my whole body.

You know that feeling of seeing a fish out of water trying to catch their breath, but they can't find the air. It's not there. That was me, gasping for air, because I was actually holding my breath most of my life and didn't even know it. My body couldn't find a safe, steady, nurturing place to land or anyone available to catch or help me land. The ground felt like it was always moving.

My highest intention spoke really loudly to me at a very young age. I didn't want anybody to feel the emotional pain and suffering that I was in, and I wanted to bring joy, light, and happiness to others. Let them know I got them, we can do this together. Because unfortunately, I've been through a lot and dealt a hard deck.

Growing up in nature was my biggest salvation. It allowed me to be free to clear my head of the past and future and get myself really present. I remember the peace, safety, and ease in my body when I found a tree that looked like a harp. I would stand in the middle of it and find calm. Then I'd go to the "Magic Rock", a huge rock I would climb really high to sit at the top and hang there for a while. Maybe that was my first meditation as a little girl. And then there were the trees that I would swing off of into a big pile of leaves. I found and created some joy and calm in the middle of all the noise.

Finding Light in the Dark

When my sister was diagnosed with breast cancer, I was so worried. (She is cancer-free and doing great.) But at the time, I wanted to do anything I could to help her and ease any discomfort. Be there for her in any way I could. Then the whole family decided to fly to where she lived to be with her, and they told me I couldn't come because there wasn't enough room for me.

Yes, I stayed home and cried and felt a lot of sad feelings. I tried to think, *It's not about me. It's about her getting well.* But it still felt very triggering and lonely. I still wanted to follow my highest intentions of helping in some way to bring light.

One day, I found another way I could help. By myself, I decided to commit to walking sixty miles in three days to raise money for breast cancer and joined the Breast Cancer Walk. When I told my family that I was going to raise money and do this, it was not received well by my mom. She asked, "Why are you doing this? Why would you do that?" instead of supporting or encouraging me.

There were other challenging times and circumstances. When I was forty-five, I got a call from my doctor during the holidays saying I had ten years worth of cancer. To say the least, I was shocked. Not having a family that supported me was really hard. And navigating special education in the school system without any support and at home had a huge effect. Then I experienced a horrible divorce. All during the pandemic!

And don't get me started with all the animals that were attacking my home, making holes in the roof, and trying to get in. All while trying to parent through it as a single mom. And sadly, my dog passed away unexpectedly. Her name was Marlo, and she was definitely my rock.

There was a lot of grief and loss and still is, but in that grief, I try to be open in small ways to see signs and synchronicities and what I call my God winks.

Reclaiming Reality

There were so many other things and events that affected me and made me feel like I couldn't breathe. I was told that it was emotional abuse, narcissism, gaslighting, and manipulation. I didn't know what those words were at the time. Now I know it's twisting of truths and questioning your reality. I was listening to everybody else's voice. I was taking in all others' unserving, unaligned actions. I wasn't able to fully embody, believe, and trust my own truth because the other voices and untrue stories were so much louder. And I didn't have anyone to help me.

I finally had to ask for help and guidance from a priest because as much as I wanted to do it on my own, I couldn't. I explained my situation to him about my family, and he said I have to remove myself from it.

"It's okay, it's okay," he said. "Sometimes you have to move away from things and family to then heal."

He allowed me and gave me permission to find some peace, truth, and ease. He explained that God doesn't want us to be unhappy or held down. I had light to give.

This was the opening when I was forty years old. I needed to hear about finding my way back to me, my inner strength, and my greatest love inside of me. (Sounds like a song you might've heard by Whitney Houston. I used to sing it at the top of my lungs in high school.)

I was starting to become aware of what was really true. My intentions, voice, and truth were getting louder, so I could hear them. I am untethering from the old identity and messages. And learning it's okay to speak up if it's hurting me and is unfair. And yes, it was maddening to not be seen and supported. My voice fell on deaf ears. There was no accountability or responsibility for actions. It's appropriate to feel anger because I was surviving on crumbs.

Aligning with Spirit

Here's the thing I notice now. Although it was hard, I listened to myself and aligned with my authentic spirit, the highest vibe of wanting to help people. For the Breast Cancer Walk, I organized a fundraising event in my home and asked for help to raise a lot of money to support those going through breast cancer. During the walk, it was so moving, connecting, and inspiring. I was surrounded by like-minded people aligned with my authentic being. And because I was there, I was able to help in another way that might not have happened.

It was May in Boston. There was a crazy, unexpected storm. It was pouring buckets of cold rain, and temperatures were so cold that many people were getting hypothermia during the walk and were taken to the hospital. Each night, we slept in tents and showered in big Mack trucks. The universe aligned that day because my home was on the route of the walk, and participants passed it. As the storm continued, we had to get off the trail. It was unsafe to keep going and sleep outside in those conditions. I was able to bring a bunch of people to my home to sleep, so they felt safe, dry, and warm. It allowed us to continue and complete the walk the next day. We made it! At the finish line, we were greeted with the loudest cheers and many tears.

During the summer and two days after Marlo passed away, my girls and I flew to Kentucky for a wedding. I was trying to focus on the positive event and not sit in my sad emotions. We were walking past a building next to our hotel, and I looked up, and there was a big sign that said "Mercury".

Wow! I thought. When we adopted Marlo from the shelter, her name was Mercury. I felt like she was there, and it was a sign from her.

Then, after the wedding, we flew home, and the next weekend, we went to a fun family restaurant we frequent in the summer. I was waiting to order something to drink at the bar, and a mom standing next to me started screaming, "Marlo, Marlo, Marlo, get over here."

I looked up in shock and asked, "What name did you just say?"

"Marlo", for her daughter, she said. I was taken aback.

These events happened within a few days of each other. I ended up going up to the mom a few minutes later and telling her why I was in shock. She thanked me for telling her, and said that she was so glad I shared that with her. It was a beautiful connection.

A week later, we were at dinner in another state, and for some reason, I asked the waitress her name.

She said, "Marlo."

No way! Yes way. Omg. The signs. I'm so glad my heart was open enough and had space to receive these God winks, or I might have missed them. I was able to receive the gift of Marlo again. So powerful. The energy all around us. I think Marlo was there with me in all these places, letting me know she was okay, letting me know that she was there for me and had my back. After all, she had been to both those places with me. I believe these were not coincidences, and they were signs, God winks, glorious synchronicities, reminding me to stay open to lead with my heart and be authentically me.

The Gift of Growth

It was just before Christmas and right before the divorce started. I was in the car with my girls, and they were playing a game on their phone that you spin and get a word that gives you a word to represent your future. They spun and got amazing uplifting words. When it was my turn, I was praying so hard for an uplifting word. But when I spun, I got the word "growth".

What? Growth? I felt so sad and deflated. It felt harsh. It was definitely not the word I was praying for. I couldn't wrap my head around what that even meant. Growth? Little did I know at that time that there was going to be enormous growth in me and for me. And there were beautiful people and aligned paths that were going to come into my life and open me up and light me up. Oh, it was painful all right and grueling.

I now know what growing pains mean and feel like. What the word "growth" offered me was so much more, the doors it opened, and by the grace of God, my continued perseverance led me to the most amazing trainer and mindfulness and emotional intelligence class. I felt so much gratitude and transformation that I became certified to coach the program.

Now I was surrounded by an aligned community of coaches, connection, elevation, empowerment, truth, trust, liberation, and understanding. I learned what self-love should be and feel like, and what was not serving me and my highest intention, and what was holding me down and keeping me away from it. And what needed to be removed so I could grow and help me see what was truly good and meant for me. I'm so grateful for growth. Since then I have committed to keep growing, expanding, relearning and giving myself lots of love and grace through it all.

Each day I remind myself I am the biggest project I will ever have, and that is my work. I'm a lifelong work in progress, doing it the best I can, at my pace, that's safe for my body. It feels really hard sometimes. I feel that resistance in my body. You know that pull that says, "Who do you think you are doing this, being seen?

That's not safe, or you can't change, you haven't changed. Let's stay the same, comfortable, low frequency because that feels safe. You might die out there!"

It has been really hard to believe, empower, and trust my beliefs, but I knew I felt so strongly in my heart and soul, of my intention of wanting to help bring joy, uplift, and encourage other people so they could soar and feel happiness.

One fun thing I did was I got myself a 'NO' button. I walk by it and hit it to stop those lies in their tracks. I've learned that's my old identity talking with lies, lies, lies. That's my addicted mind and monster playing mind tricks, by lying and saying it's safe to stay sad and hurt and believing the lies and staying unseen in the same patterns because that's comfortable. That's all you know.

But that is not who you are. It isn't even your own words or stories. It's from somebody else. And you don't have to keep carrying those stories. They are not your stories, beliefs, or truths. They try to hijack you back into the lowest energy and keep you there exhausted, so you can't move towards your highest intention and healthiest self.

Yes, it's that itty bitty committee. I didn't have any tools that said I could change the station and create new neural pathways toward my new identity and truths, and have that stick and grow and get louder. Those are so much wiser and tell the truth.

As I grow, I practice not abandoning and betraying myself by not listening to others' lies and stories. I've learned to trust my truth, learn about what my truth is, and my intuition, and my inner wisdom. I get to change the radio station to my highest frequency. Let's go!

I also get to notice and see what I always knew. My intuition was speaking loudly, but I wasn't able to hear it or let it lead me because the old identity was leading and was so loud and strong. I get to let go of what's not aligned and serving me to reach my highest intention and capabilities.

I get to give myself lots of grace, a reset, and keep committing regardless of what the old identity says. I give my nervous system love, first, with full, gentle breaths in and slowly out, and ease any tension in my body to allow myself to keep on reconnecting to my highest self.

One of the most powerful things I've learned is that my body and nervous system need me to notice when it's feeling dysregulated, so I can give it what it needs to get back to feeling ease, safety, calm, and clarity. Putting my hand on my heart, I take in slow, gentle breaths and move out energy that is not serving me so I make space for clarity and ease.

When I'm feeling low or I think I haven't made progress, I look at the big pines in my backyard, and they remind me of my growth and expansion. Even when I can't feel it or see it, it's happening. I realize I can't see the trees growing every day, but they are, and they put down deep roots to hold them up and expand and spread them. Slow, steady, and reaching for the light, and weathering storms, and reaching for the sun to be nourished and be grounded, and give me oxygen so I can breathe and be alive. Wow.

Coming Back Home to Me

I have people in my life who I really want to be there for me, support me, and love me, but are just unavailable. It's been the hardest thing for me to learn. But I continue to keep learning and growing. I'm committed to creating space to be open so I can receive and experience people who are available and aligned with my spirit, love, and light.

I'm grateful for this practice. It's a gift, and like medicine, I give myself every day to get stronger to help me break through old beliefs, identities, and patterns of abandoning me and betraying me, so I can nourish and feed my soul and intention with grace and love. I get to live it and share it.

So I'm shaking it up and out. Coming back home to me, to my love and light of that cute little bambino who was meant to shine with bright light and love into the world.

I was recently looking out my living room window, and right outside were two little boys walking and talking together, and one of them tripped over a stick and fell on his face. Instead of crying, he started laughing, and then he picked up the stick and put it down in front of him again and pretended to trip and fall on his face. Then the boys looked at each other, and started laughing hysterically and sprinted off. I loved seeing that because I needed that reminder that, yes, there are going to be real obstacles in life and, yes, we are going to trip, and then learn, yes, we can handle it.

We get to trip again and again and again and ask for help when we need it, and then we get to laugh again because we are going to be okay, and we can create new friendships and joy and skip and run off laughing together, too.

Lost and Found

HOW A HEALING CRISIS REWROTE MY PLAYBOOK

Cheri Fredrickson

I had always been healthy and athletic. I took great comfort in this and relied on my physicality to manage my life. I loved running for problem-solving and experiencing time in nature. I loved racing sailboats for the excitement, challenge, and camaraderie of working with others to accomplish a goal. I loved hiking and backpacking to keep things in perspective. Problems seemed much smaller when standing on top of a mountain looking at a beautiful vista. And I loved dancing for connecting with other people while listening to good music.

Yes, my body had served me well. It was a good friend and ally. Until it wasn't.

One day, I went for a long hike with a friend. Coming home very tired after a long day in the hot sun, I fell asleep on the couch without cleaning up or changing out of my grubby clothes. I stayed there until morning, and when I hopped in the shower, I noticed a couple of unusual things on my body. There were two dark lumps with legs.

I immediately jumped online and started looking up what they might be. Deer ticks.

Okay. I didn't live in an area that was known for things like Lyme disease, so I wasn't too concerned. I looked up how to get them out, did what I needed to do, put them in the freezer in case they needed to be tested, and went about my day. I was totally grossed out at having had to remove bugs from my body, but I was no worse for wear. Or so I thought.

It wasn't long before I noticed a round rash expanding around one of the bites, and I started feeling like I had the flu. I headed to my naturopath, who referred me to a Lyme specialist. She put me on doxycycline and assured me that it would take care of it since I had caught it quickly. We sent the critters off for testing, and I also took a test. Both positive. And, even after a few weeks, the doctor wasn't solving the problem. The offered solution? More doxy.

I wasn't too keen on that because I was aware of what long-term use of antibiotics can do to your gut microbiome, as well as your immunity. I decided to look for other answers and keep this as a last resort.

I searched, I read, I asked around, I meditated, I prayed, and I got worse. But it kind of came in waves, and during a wave when I felt better, I decided to do a little dating and signed up on a dating site. I only went on two dates, but one dramatically changed the course of my illness. The man I met up with was well-versed in plant medicine and wanted to give me a book. He didn't know about my Lyme disease; he just thought I'd really like it. It turned out to be *The Secret Teachings of Plants* by Stephen Harrod Buhner.

He was right. I loved the book. I've always had an interest in plant medicine, and I found the author's relationship with plants fascinating, particularly his teachings about allowing them to guide you in their use. Imagine my surprise to find out the author was an internationally recognized Lyme specialist. I ordered his book, *Healing Lyme,* and reached out to learn more. I started his protocol right away and, while I didn't notice a big change immediately, my intuition told me I was on the right path.

An Unlikely Request

Even though I eventually started feeling better, I continued to feel frustrated at my loss of physical abilities and ongoing pain. For quite some time, I hadn't been able to do many of the things that brought me joy. I had lost strength, coordination, ability to focus, and endurance. Doing physical activities wasn't fun anymore. My body hurt. Sometimes a lot. I missed being active so much, and I didn't know what to do.

So, I meditated. And, in meditation, I asked for a solution. I spoke to the Universe, expressing my displeasure with my quality of life. I let the "Higher Ups" know that if this was what my life had in store for me, I was perfectly fine with it being over. And, if they wanted me to stick around, I needed some answers. I needed to know how to get my life back. I heard one word, loud and clear: *Nia*.

My response? "You've got to be kidding."

I knew a little bit about Nia and had friends who did it. I had gone to a couple of classes years before. It was kind of flowy and free-form. I was definitely more linear as a runner, a rower, a sailor, and a rider. I had never been drawn to it. But I was desperate. I began looking for classes, but couldn't find any that fit my life. Good grief!

More meditation and conversation. "If you want me to do Nia, the least you can do is make it accessible. I need to find a class I can go to."

Again, I heard one word, loud and clear: *Teach*.

That was even more laughable to me. I couldn't imagine I would be any good at teaching Nia, or that anyone would want to go to my classes. I have never, ever had a desire to teach movement classes. But I was still desperate, so I reached out to learn how to teach.

As it turned out, the local white belt classes (necessary for teaching) were not being offered because Nia headquarters was developing Nia TV. I did find an upcoming training course a few hours away. Whew! It turned out to be a split class, making it much easier for me physically. I still hurt, and I didn't have much stamina. Knowing I would have a break in the middle between two long weekends relieved some of my anxiety about attending, so I signed up.

It didn't take me long to realize that this was much more than a physical practice. Nia incorporates mental, emotional, physical, and spiritual realms. I also learned that it was developed to promote healing along with fitness. The creators used to own an aerobics business in the Bay Area. They noticed that traditional aerobics often led to injuries, particularly from the knee down. They believed there had to be a way to become fit without injuring oneself.

Because of that, they made it their mission to develop a practice that promoted healing along with fitness. They studied many movement forms and settled on fifty-two moves, drawing from martial arts (Tai Chi, Taekwondo, and Aikido), dance arts (Jazz, Modern, and Duncan Dance), and healing arts (the work of Moshe Feldenkrais, the Alexander Technique, and Yoga). It was exactly what I needed. The combination of movements, along with the four aspects of being, combined to promote a level of healing that far exceeded my expectations. Not only was I able to heal from Lyme disease, but I was also able to heal injuries from years ago.

One of the fundamental tenets of Nia is, "Now I am self-healing." I said that to myself repeatedly, every day. Another important aspect was one of the principles: "Joy of Movement." I learned I could access the joy of movement no matter how I was feeling or what my abilities were. What a game changer!

During my white belt training, I had one particularly odd experience. I began to have profound itching in the area where the infected tick had bitten me. I had experienced this before, but this time it had a different quality. It increased in intensity, and then, quite suddenly, it left. It felt almost as if tentacles were leaving my body. I knew, at that moment, I would never experience it again. And, many years later, I still haven't.

The Next Step

My white belt training had me feeling noticeably better physically, but I was still terrified at the thought of teaching. I had no real background in Nia, or dance fitness, and the thought put me so far out of my comfort zone that I couldn't even see it.

Then came the great news: There's a green belt specifically focused on teaching.

I'm in! Only one problem. They are shutting the training down to be revamped. There was only one more happening. As it turns out, the last green belt was being offered in Montana, forty-five minutes from our ranch, and it started a day after I would be at a ranch for a family meeting. Coincidence? I don't think so.

Green belt training was everything I imagined and more. It prepared me well to begin teaching, although I was still profoundly nervous and dealing with issues from Lyme disease. When I started teaching, I can remember songs coming on and thinking, *I've never heard this before.* It wasn't true, but my brain was still healing. And, somehow, I made it through.

Venues showed up for me to get started teaching classes. I had a beautiful studio available for free for the first several months. Then a lovely ballroom became available. People came. I healed. They healed. It was lovely. I was able to rebuild my coaching practice, and life settled back into an easy rhythm.

This all prepared me for the next step in my journey. Just as I was regaining my own strength, life asked me to be strong for someone else. I stepped into the role of caring for my mother in her decline. At first, I was traveling back and forth to where she lived, about an hour and a half away. Eventually, I chose to move in with her so she could stay at home. I had cared for my dad in his last years, so I thought I knew what I was getting into. However, I was unprepared for some of the challenges that showed up with the loss of the second parent.

Shortly before my mother passed, my eldest brother passed away. He did not have a will, which created estate issues concerning our family ranch business. Our mom wanted to cover the cost of those issues, but she did not put it in writing, and she was unable to oversee the financial piece before she passed. One of my remaining siblings was quite adamant that we did not have to honor our mother's wishes now that she was gone. We argued. A lot.

Fortunately, I had learned, through my experience with Lyme, to ask for the guidance I wanted and needed. In addition to the family challenges, she passed away at the same time we entered the COVID-19 lockdown. I found myself isolated in a town where I didn't know many people, dealing with all the things that go with the death of a loved one, such as estate hassles, and her home and possessions. I ended up staying there, purchasing the house, and slowly working through all of it.

Head and Heart

I wouldn't say it was an easy chapter in my life, but I felt strongly led in my process. A tremendous amount of healing occurred during that time. Because of my own stress level, I sought out tools that led me to HeartMath®, a system of scientifically validated techniques and technologies designed to help people manage stress, become more resilient, and improve overall well-being through heart-brain synchronization. I had such profoundly positive results, including better sleep, calmer presence when dealing with the family, and a greater sense of ease, that I chose to become certified as a coach/mentor and trainer with them.

I was also able to deepen my learning with the teachings of Jack Canfield and have enjoyed and benefited from his work for decades. One of my favorite books is *The Success Principles*, and I love sharing these simple yet powerful tools with others.

When the time was right, I asked for more guidance on where to land when I no longer wanted to be in my parents' old home. I made a list of what mattered to me in choosing a new place to live, and Eugene, Oregon, checked all the boxes.

Moving there fell into place so easily. I found my condo in one trip, without looking at any other homes. I live in a beautiful place in the forest where I have access to miles of walking trails outside my door, and I often describe myself as being hugged by trees. I love my neighbors and my community. It was definitely meant to be.

The combination of personal challenges, guidance, and learning has brought me to this next stage of my life, where I'm bringing it all together. I now offer coaching and training that helps others learn to create coherence between heart and mind, allowing them to integrate the strengths of each type of thinking. For me, I often find that my intuitive heart sense shows me what's next, and my mental process helps me determine how to make that a reality.

I used to rely on my thought processes for goal-setting, creating a plan, everything, really. It often worked well for me. But, it was also effortful, and there were times when my plans turned out to be more of what I thought I "should" do than what was ultimately right for me. My results often lacked joy, even though I got good results by typical standards.

What I've learned is that life is far easier and more joyful when we allow ourselves to be led and use all of the tools available to us. For most of us, that involves some healing and creating new pathways in the brain, as well as learning how to listen to the messages our bodies are sharing.

When we listen to what our body communicates, we can access more information, which ultimately leads to choices that are aligned with our higher good. We are more connected with our purpose. This also leads to a greater sense of ease and satisfaction with the choices we make. We tend to be drawn to the right people and circumstances, leading to even more ease and satisfaction. It is such a joy!

When we become familiar with our emotions, where we're holding tension, subtle energy shifts, body sensations, health issues, etc., they all become like good friends there to provide information that leads us where we most need to go.

For me, it begins with heart-focused breathing. Whatever is happening in my life, if I begin with breathing that is focused in the area of my heart, I am quickly in a better place to tackle whatever comes next. I often choose to add a positive or renewing feeling. I don't do this to negate the importance of my other emotions, but to shift into a place that is more conducive to effective action. Often, when we make decisions or take action from a negative or depleting emotion, we make choices that are not in our best interests. All emotions have value, and the tough ones show us where we may need to course-correct. But they generally don't lead us to the choices and actions that are best for us.

Adding movement can deepen the learning. I find that when I dance my emotions, or tap into areas of my body that are holding tension through movement or meditation, I can gather more information. I often get insights that I didn't have before, leading to better outcomes than I likely would have had without them. Sometimes I ask directly for what I want to know. Sometimes I just allow whatever wants to show up to appear. Both ways have their gifts.

Listening to my body supports me in having a clear sense of what comes next when I'm working with clients. I find they are also better able to determine what is right for them when they learn to interpret the messages from their bodies. Additional tools like HeartMath® and The Success Principles provide the structure that makes their goals and desires come alive, and that kind of structure makes it easier for most people to implement. There is also an element of comfort in having a known methodology, as long as we are not overly rigid in our use of the tools.

An Invitation

As you reflect on this chapter, I invite you to consider:

Where might your body be trying to get your attention?

What wisdom have you been overriding with effort or logic alone?

What might become possible if you allowed yourself to listen more deeply and honor what your body wants you to know?

Begin simply. Place a hand on your heart. Take a few slow, intentional breaths. Notice what your body is trying to tell you before you decide what comes next.

Your body knows the way forward. Your mind helps you figure out how to make it happen.

We are all richer each time another person taps into their purpose and shares it with the world. All of us are here to make a difference in some way. May you know the joy of experiencing and expressing your uniqueness!

Mixed Messages

Finding My Voice After Years of Hiding

Kim Carter

What if the thing you were labeled for your entire life wasn't your weakness but the very thing that shaped who you became? One day, my father told me to "Stop being so sensitive." It felt like a demand, and I immediately told myself it wasn't safe to be me.

However, I didn't grow up "being too sensitive." I grew up learning how to survive emotional chaos. My life has been a roller coaster of emotions ever since I can remember, and for a long time, I thought that meant something was wrong with me.

As a little girl, I never wanted to go to school because I didn't want to leave my mom. Home was safe and comfortable. Mine.

Eventually, I had to start school. While I went to kindergarten without issues, when it was time for first grade, things changed. I hated it. I remember thinking my teacher was mean, and I had zero interest in learning anything she was teaching.

The only part of school I loved was getting new clothes. My parents took my siblings and me to the Sears department store, and getting to choose my own clothes made me feel in control. A new outfit made me feel like I could handle the day, but what I didn't know then was that I was using clothes like armor in a battle I was already losing.

Looking back, that should have been my first clue. I wasn't avoiding school. I was trying to regulate/control how the world made me feel.

First grade was where things really went hard for me. I didn't learn how to read. No matter how much my mom and dad tried to help, it just wasn't clicking. I can picture sitting at the kitchen table, night after night, staring at the words, feeling my frustration grow, and watching theirs grow too.

I wanted to get it. I believe I really did, but I couldn't.

To this day, I'm not sure if learning felt hard or if I had already decided it wasn't for someone like me.

Learning to Hide

Somewhere between those flashcards and that kitchen table, I started to believe that trying harder didn't always mean succeeding. I didn't think something was wrong with me, but I just couldn't figure out why I couldn't read.

I ended up failing the first grade.

The moment I realized I had failed came on the last day of school. I was riding home on the bus, surrounded by kids smiling and laughing, pulling their report cards out of their backpacks. Everyone was excited, calling out what grade they were going into next.

"I'm going into second grade."

"I'm going into third grade."

I couldn't read my report card, so I turned to the sweet girl next to me and asked if she would read it to me. She said yes. I handed it to her and watched as she began reading.

Right in the middle of her sentence, she paused and said, "I think your parents should read it to you." I didn't understand why, but I didn't question her, I just said, "Okay."

Not knowing what any of it meant yet, I ran in the house and handed my report card to my mom. She took the report card from my hands and sat down. I stood there watching her as she unfolded it. Her eyes moved across the page slowly, carefully. I remember studying her face, waiting for her reaction.

Then she looked up at me. She did not look happy at all. She looked concerned. Her voice was soft and gentle, even a little hurt because she knew what she was about to tell me. My excitement disappeared, and a sensation of dread filled my body.

She told me that I wasn't moving on to second grade. That I would be repeating first. I didn't cry or argue. I don't even remember asking questions. I ran around to the back of the house and hid.

You see, that was the first time I wanted to hide myself from the world, but not the last.

The Second Time Around

The next part of my story gets even better. When I was a little older, I knocked out all four of my baby teeth, running full speed into a parked car. Yes, a parked car. When my adult teeth finally came in, they came in buck and spaced out. It was so bad that I could barely close my mouth.

Then, later that same school year, my dad decided my long, blonde hair had to go. And just like that, it was chopped into a short pixie cut. I walked out of the salon on Saturday looking like a boy. On Monday, my classroom made sure I knew it!

Before I could even find my seat, a boy yelled, "Who's the new boy in the class?"

Who's the new boy in the class? It echoed in my head, and my body went hot. My stomach dropped. And just like that, the room told me who I was.

So, I hid. I climbed into that musty-smelling coat closet and stayed there until my teacher gently pulled me out. That was the moment I learned that when you don't feel like you belong, your first instinct is to disappear. In that coat closet, I didn't just hide from my classmates, I hid from myself.

However, that coat closet wasn't just a hiding place. It was where I learned how quickly shame teaches us to shrink. I didn't know it then, but that coat closet would teach me the opposite lesson over the next thirty years, how much courage it takes to take up space again.

After that day, I didn't suddenly become invisible, but I did become careful. I learned how to read a room before ever learning how to read a book. I figured out which parts of myself I could safely let be seen and which parts were better tucked away. I learned how to smile without showing my teeth. And I learned how to be quiet enough not to draw attention, but to be pleasant enough to be liked.

Hiding, I discovered, wasn't always literal. Sometimes it looked like blending in, being easy, softening my voice, shrinking my thoughts, or staying quiet even when I had something to say.

The thing about hiding is that it works, at least for a while.

When hiding, I avoided embarrassment and judgment, that warm sensation in your body that says, everyone is looking at you. Hiding keeps you safe. At least it feels like it does.

So, I kept doing it all through school, and I became good at staying under the radar.

What looked healed on the outside still needed time on the inside.

Out of the Shadows

Eventually, I got braces on my teeth, and I was able to grow my hair long again. I still remember the day my braces came off. I looked in the mirror and couldn't stop smiling. My hair fell all the way down my back, a golden brown that caught the sunlight.

For the first time, I felt beautiful. The boys noticed. The girls did too. They liked my style and the way I carried myself with attitude.

But changing outside was much easier than changing what was happening on the inside. While I looked fine on the surface, I was still carrying emotional scars I didn't yet know how to heal. And that's where I continued to struggle.

There was another moment, years later, that hit just as hard, even though it didn't happen in a classroom. It happened at home.

One day, my friend, who lived across the street from me, and I were arguing. I was upset and told my mother about it. My mother said something to me that I've never forgotten.

She stated, "You don't get along with anybody."

It felt like a gut punch. I almost believed her because when it comes from your mother, you tend to believe it. For a second, it made me question everything I thought I knew about myself. But something different happened this time. Instead of shrinking, I paused. Then, instinctively, I rejected it.

I replied, "That's not true." I said it out loud with conviction, even though I was ready to cry. Deep down, I knew something she couldn't see at that moment: I did get along with others. I always had. Connection had never been my issue, confidence had.

At the time, that moment mattered more than I had realized.

It was the first time I chose my own knowing over someone else's narrative. It was the first time I hadn't automatically absorbed a statement about who I was and made it my identity.

It would have been easy to let her opinion become another reason to hide. Another label to live under. Another unspoken rule. You don't fit in. You're too difficult.

Instead, I challenged it.

And that challenge cracked me wide open.

Staying True

Speaking up for myself showed me confidence isn't always built by praise. Sometimes it's built by refusal. It can look like saying, no, that's not my truth, and recognizing when someone else's words are about their lens rather than your reality.

That moment didn't magically heal everything, and I didn't walk away with a ton of self-confidence, but I was better able to figure out for myself what felt true and what did not.

I started to understand that not every voice deserves authority over your identity. Not every opinion gets to become a belief, and not every painful statement is meant to be carried.

That realization became another step out of the closet because hiding often starts when we accept someone else's definition of us without question. Confidence grows when we learn to ask, *Is that true?*

For the first time, I trusted myself enough to answer.

Looking back to that day in school, hiding in the coat closet, I learned how to shrink, but I would spend the rest of my life learning how to take up space again.

I had to learn to trust myself and believe in myself because I couldn't always find that in others.

However, that realization didn't come easily. While my life was not all gloom and doom, this experience is an honest look at some of the challenges I faced and how they shaped the way I saw myself.

This isn't about placing blame or pointing fingers. It's about acknowledging how easily we absorb other people's words, internalize them as truth, and carry them with us into the future, often without realizing the weight they hold.

As I got older and lived through more of life's lessons, I finally understood that self-confidence is not something anyone else can give you. It's something you give yourself.

Confidence doesn't come from approval or applause, or someone believing in you first; it starts from the inside out.

Here's the best part: This is an incredible realization. When you're the one who gives it to yourself, no one can ever take it away from you.

Meaningful Connections

As an adult and my career evolved, I spent thirteen years teaching in a classroom. One year changed everything, the year I helped kindergarteners learn how to read.

Sitting with those children felt personal because their struggles reminded me of my own. The same fear and pressure to keep up radiated through the room. Helping them learn to read felt like reaching back in time and finally giving my younger self what she needed.

Teaching those children to read wasn't just helping them learn letters and sounds. I was rewriting my own story and healing the deep wounds that started in first grade.

Over the years, I've also become someone who naturally builds connections everywhere I go. I've met people on airplanes, in store parking lots, and in department stores. I've had meaningful conversations with CEOs in elevators and strangers standing next to me in line.

What I've learned is that connection doesn't care about titles, status, or where you meet; it only requires presence. It didn't matter where we were or who they were. It mattered that I showed up open and curious.

Growing up, I didn't always feel comfortable talking to people. In fact, this skill grew alongside my confidence. The more I practiced connecting with others, the more I trusted myself. I learned how to start conversations, how to listen, and how to genuinely care about someone else's story. I asked questions and paid attention. And when it felt right, I followed up.

Now, I feel comfortable talking to anyone, anywhere. I see it as an opportunity. I've even turned it into a personal challenge: how many people can I learn about today? That mindset shifts everything because when the focus is on curiosity instead of self-consciousness, confidence follows.

This is the foundation of the work I do today. Confidence grows when you trust yourself enough to connect, and connection deepens when you stop trying to impress and start trying to understand. That combination has changed my life, and it's what I help others build every day.

Think about a time when someone has said something about you that never felt aligned with who you really are. Did you internalize it, or did you reject it? Or maybe there was a time when you felt like hiding. Did you hide or have the courage to be seen?

What I've learned from others is simple but powerful. When you show genuine interest in someone else, when you listen without an agenda and ask questions because you truly want to understand, a connection happens naturally. There is no script or strategy. Just human-to-human interaction, and that's where the magic happens.

Returning to Wild

A Journey to Gently Reclaim the Wild Girl Within

Heather Campbell

The Catalpa opens her branches, and I climb as high as I dare. Dense leaves hide me from the dreary house and the yelling inside. My fingers trace the wrinkled bark. I am safe in the tree's arms.

My brother slams the door and walks ahead. I climb down and follow behind, making up songs, pocketing pretty rocks, and rescuing earthworms that crept onto the sidewalk after the rain.

At school, I'm "intelligent but different," the odd favorite who stays after to tidy or weave stories of my make-believe farm. The teachers know I live near the tracks where the trains shake my window, singing noisy lullabies at night.

Most days, the dread of going home takes me on different journeys. I cautiously cross barbed wire through pastures or new subdivisions that rise from old corn-fields. In a field of feral horses, I gaze at mountains that band the horizon and imagine running away. Plucking some grass, I stretch my arm toward a mare in the field. Ears twitch, she watches me, then she approaches.

Childhood sways from laughter to violence. My dad lovingly takes us skiing or on camping trips, then flips furniture in a rage as I cower under the bed. Uncertainty sharpens my hypervigilance. I become a chameleon, tiptoeing and fawning, taking storms into my body. I adapt to instability by smoothing conflict, cleaning the house, watching my tone, and bracing for impact.

My parents' turbulent marriage detonates. A blurred memory of my bruised mother, a rushed escape, and tires skidding toward safety. Months later, my dad "finds Jesus," and we join a small church. For a while, there is closeness, even peace. But another storm gathers with messages in tongues, an angry God, and shame that roots deep. I learn my heart is deceitful and my body is sinful, making salvation precarious. I pray hard, try harder, and wear perfection like armor.

In high school, anxiety takes hold.

Hands press down on my head. Fierce whispers hiss, "Yessss, Jesus-s-s-s."

Someone here has displeased the Lord. It's me again, in the center of the prayer circle. Teachers tell me I'm gifted, while my church tells me I'm defective. I captain the swim team, earn scholarships, and graduate with honors, but these are labeled prideful. My father frowns at my cap and gown and calls graduation a "parade of iniquity."

When I struggle for air at university swim practice, a doctor misdiagnoses panic attacks as exercise-induced asthma, and prescriptions worsen symptoms. Swimming allows me an escape and a sense of purpose, but I'm suffocating from fear and shame.

"Your dad told me to tell you, sweetheart," my mother says gently over the phone. "It was revealed to Pastor Bob that college and swimming are not the Lord's perfect will for you."

I shatter. Every cell dissents, but I have no choice. The coil of guilt tightens around my chest and throat. I must obey.

Depression settles in as purpose fades, so I pack my tiny car and wander. I sleep in the resort parking lot beneath quiet snow, on forest roads by the climbing walls I love, and near the university I stray from and return to. The mountains quiet me. University lectures inspire me. For years, I drift between hopelessness and the girl who is alive, safe, and uniquely herself.

Aimlessly, I flirt with academia and adventures. Between moments in the mountains, I meander through college until enough credits are gathered into a major.

A Smile Suspends Me

We fall fast in love, and my plans dissolve. Red flags unfurl, and I dismiss them. Shame about intimacy propels us to elope in the park where I used to practice guitar between classes. The early years are magic. We adventure through Colorado mountains, take river trips, and work at a Utah national park. I share wild dreams of mountain life with him, unaware of his desire for concrete and routine.

When I become pregnant, he takes a job at a retail box store for insurance and security. Dreams of adventure and travel slowly fade. The wild girl steps aside as the perfectionist emerges.

My son arrives, then my daughter. Love emanates and engulfs me. My children are my compass and my heart. The perfectionist excels at playing house, and motherhood replaces any former desire to escape. Service, expectations, and routine keep me too busy to notice the subtle changes in myself and my marriage.

Years twist around us. I begin to feel the slow strangle of tendrils. Depression, substance abuse, neglect, and a thousand other micro-abuses become ever more visible. I give and care without reciprocity until I am gradually scraped hollow.

I ask women at my Bible study how to make my husband happy. They tell me, "Submit more. Pray more. Serve, smile, and sex more." The responsibility is solely mine, so I bear it until my body cannot.

My hand dabs a washcloth on his sweating forehead. Slow weeks of OxyContin withdrawals take hold. I steady myself and find a smile to safeguard my children from the situation upstairs.

Health returns, promises are made, and we resume. Then, infidelity and unmistakable deception, the futility of my sacrifices makes me retch. Ebbs and flows of wooing me back follow reasons to leave. He finds footholds in the cracks of my boundaries and worms back into our lives through dinner, a foot rub, and a kiss. I flee across state lines, then return, dismissing my intuition. Hoping for kept promises, threats of suicide keep me hostage.

Into the Darkness

My nervous system begs for a pause, and a chance opportunity invites one. The mountain air at the winter camp I'm chaperoning stirs something inside. The pine fragrance and innumerable stars intoxicate my senses, rousing the wild girl. I'm fully present. I feel what enlivens me and recognize how dead I've been.

Pain seduces me. What if I vanish into the forest and let the moss and humus consume me?

If I close my eyes and let go, maybe I could leave the heartache and exit this cycle of mistakes. The tether of my children pulls me back. I would never, could never, leave them.

Returning from camp, my body unexpectedly responds when one morning I wake up and can't move from excruciating pain and unimaginable swelling. Symptoms dismissed by doctors over the years flare into severe rheumatoid arthritis. Simple movements become nearly impossible overnight. My body reaches a full stop.

Over the next few months, the slightest brush or bump sends fire and knives into my joints. I breathe through the pain to get through daily tasks. Frustrated by diminished household duties and bedroom intimacy, he shoves me in the back one night, "I can't have you like this. You need to figure this out."

In this instant, I abruptly recognize the neglected truth that I am alone. In the anguished darkness, this realization provides a pinpoint of light. Clarity guides me forward into a new story, and I finally leave.

Survival is necessary, but love is my power. It surges between waves of heartache and resilience. I tumble through this transition. The haze of pain obscures memory, but my children are a lighthouse. Love strengthens me as I navigate doctors, career, finances, and decisions.

Choosing a Path

"Happy birthday!"

I gape in confusion at the closing agent. She hands my license back, smiling. Truly having forgotten my birthday, I kindly thank her and pause in awe.

Signature after signature, I sign and date the last page, caressing my aching hand. On my birthday, I have just closed on an adorable home outside of town. Bursting with gratitude, I exit the title company, tears spilling down my cheeks as I whisper skyward, "Thank you."

The sunrise blushes with soft pinks and orange. Chickens greet me with lively clucks, and ducks quack nearby. I gather eggs into the pocket of my jacket, my joints still tender but healing.

I've expertly navigated outer storms, but an inner one gathers.

The goats bolt from their enclosure. I adore them, but they have decimated hard work in the garden. The decision to rehome them has been made because there isn't adequate space for them here. The man is aggressive and handles them roughly. At once, I regret my decision, but I'm frozen as he drives away while the terrified goats bleat.

The chaotic scene agitates deeply buried pain. Infection surfaces, and I burst open. Every hurt from father, brother, pastor, and husband surges out of me. I collapse and wail until exhausted. My defenses crumble. The rubble of willpower in pieces around me, I am uncertain how to move forward.

In the pew, I nodded solemnly at sermons of shame for decades, believing that my unworthy heart was wretched and deceptive. Now, the wild girl wrestles under gripping tangles of condemnation, shame, and fear. Therapy and mental health were stigmatized in my religious upbringing, but I am desperate. I reach for help.

Buzzers pulse between each hand. My voice catches through tears as I recount stories. My body shakes, breaths jagged.

The therapist speaks softly, "Float." Instantly, I'm on my back in the waters of a lake from memory.

She pulls me into this moment when I dysregulate, slowing the buzzers' pulse. When I steady, she invites me to resume. Her gentle guidance allows me to feel each emotion and honor my truth. During our sessions, value is unlinked from productivity and busyness. Emotions are allowed to flow. Tears, laughter, rest, and play show up at their perfect time.

Imposter syndrome clamors from the periphery. Hyperindependence and insecurity clash. Anxiety perches on my shoulders. Dissociation tempts me to construct a shell, and depression lulls me inside. These guardians materialize as I flounder with new skills and understanding. Balancing gratitude and space from my protectors, I work to rewire old programming. Nervous system regulation and mindful practices are daily rituals. Growth is arduous but steady.

Reiki sessions help unlock energy as golden warmth bathes tender joints. My throat unclenches, and I gradually find my voice. Inspired, I pursue other somatic healing modalities: Shiatsu, Internal Family Systems (IFS), and Emotional Freedom Technique (tapping), each with a guide who helps me orient at precise moments.

The Wild Reimerges

Rocky peaks embrace a tree-lined meadow. We veer into the trees and up, just one more steep mile. Soft rain settles the dust on the trail. Clouds break, and sunlight illuminates each drop. The backpack feels lighter as the mountain lake comes into view. I breathe heavily, legs trembling, but senses high. My friend and I drop our packs and set up camp, relishing the quiet.

The edge of a ski in powder, the touch of sandstone, and the rhythm of the ocean have drawn out the wild girl. Touches of grey and crow's feet display her age, but she is ever playful. She now knows trips to the desert, mountains, and coast are sacred.

At the coast, I sit beneath moss-covered trees and blooming rhododendrons, using pencils or acrylics as my medium. Observing the motion of clouds or hues of light on leaves, I settle into the slowness and connectedness of nature. Artwork complete, I rise and walk barefoot down the soft humus path to the beach. The cold Pacific waves gather around my ankles, then retreat. Time in nature has become integral to my health, creativity is medicine, and rest is vitality.

Past experiences fertilize the garden I tend. As trust and gratitude are nurtured, shame dissolves. Observing trauma with curiosity, I am fascinated by our capacities for metamorphosis and equally awed by nature's restorative power.

The spiral outward begins from within. I honor my highest self with daily practices and micro-rituals that keep me attuned and safeguard my peace—yoga, nourishment, mindfulness. Nature continues to ground and center me. These practices provide a winding journey of imperfect refinement. I'm an enthusiastic student of wellness, nutrition, and mindfulness. Guided by healers, I'm inspired to do the same for others, and this desire steers my path toward health coaching.

I have circled back to all the things I love, like painting, skiing, backpacking, and climbing. I've even taken up new active and creative hobbies, including surfing and writing in my fifties. Setbacks, flare-ups, old patterns, and anxiety still occur. But now, when struggles arrive, I pause, breathe, and offer kindness to myself.

What are these moments teaching me? What does my truest, wildest self need at this moment?

I release force and surrender to flow.

Creating my new life and untangling old beliefs has taken time. I've learned to replace agonizing, emotional effort with simplicity, leaning into what resonates with my heart and honors my body. I notice what drains and what replenishes, and loosen my grip on what I cannot control. I speak softly to the fear that once gripped me, and thank it for its intention to protect.

I welcome the wild child in the catalpa tree and invite her back to me. She still makes up songs and rescues stray earthworms. We are exactly where we need to be. Every difficult and joyful part of this path guides us. It's a twisting, sacred way.

Today is a new day to take a calming breath, lead with my authentic heart, and take another step to return to my wild.

Ascend To Your Peak

CLIMBING BACK AFTER EVERY FALL

Lori Soper

I am a three-time breast cancer survivor.

The first time I was diagnosed with breast cancer, I was forty-two years old. My children were five and seven. My cancer was discovered during a routine gynecological visit and breast exam. My oncologist shared with me that my diagnosis was just "unfortunate bad luck." I only had one risk factor for breast cancer, which was having my first child at age thirty-five.

My cancer was estrogen receptor positive, meaning that it proliferated in the presence of estrogen. Even though my cancer was stage zero, the tumor itself was considered aggressive. Treatment included a lumpectomy, radiation treatment, and five years of the drug tamoxifen. I also had to endure monthly shots of a capsule in my abdomen to stop ovulation and the resulting estrogen spike.

What I remember most about that time was driving to daily radiation treatments in challenging weather conditions, ice and snow, but I couldn't miss one. I also remember that even though my husband and I were so careful about what we discussed in front of the kids, both developed signs of anxiety. One of my children began sucking on his shirt all day long, and the other one would not let go of my hand. He just needed the reassurance of touch. I would literally have to drive with my left hand and reach into the back seat to hold his hand in the back seat of the car. My friends brought meals for my family, and we hugged and tried not to cry each time one was delivered. I specifically remember one of my close friends taking my seven-year-old to his end-of-season soccer party because I couldn't attend. I had amazing support.

My risk of recurrence was determined to be twenty percent, meaning chemotherapy was on the horizon for me. Fortunately, a new test—Oncotype DX—had been recently developed. This test analyzed the actual tumor and determined the risk of recurrence. I was told that if my risk of recurrence was below ten percent based on this test, the oncologist would not have to recommend chemotherapy. Something I was told at the time, which really stuck with me, was that if there are one hundred women with a twenty percent risk of recurrence, all of them get treated, meaning that eighty percent of them are treated unnecessarily with chemotherapy.

Read that again.

All I could think was, *I am so happy and blessed that my score came back low, and I do not need chemotherapy.*

Additionally, my oncologist, who was ahead of her time, had a discussion with me about lifestyle habits to prevent recurrence of breast cancer. She touched on nutrition, movement, and—interestingly to me at the time—a positive attitude to support healing and help prevent recurrence. I have always been a positive person and a master reframer because I can find the silver lining in anything. Even though I already had a positive attitude, I didn't truly understand how it would help me heal. I learned that later.

Sadly, and ironically, given my low risk of recurrence, my cancer recurred twice.

Just Keep Moving

I have always been a mover. I grew up dancing and danced in a professional company during my college years. After college, I started running and taking indoor cycling classes. I always felt that if I were moving and looked fit, I was healthy. Being diagnosed with cancer with only one risk factor really challenged that belief. I had to make some changes.

I took my oncologist's words to heart and made changes to my lifestyle. She gave me some specific information about a cancer prevention eating style, and I tried to incorporate those foods into my family's meals.

After recovering from surgery and radiation treatments, I worked my way back to my running routine and even began the sport of Taekwondo, earning my way to a third-degree black belt over eleven years. Don't mess with me!

I kept my positive attitude and can remember looking back on the first diagnosis as a little foothill that was behind me.

A year or two into my recovery, I was advised that my oncologist had discovered that I lacked an enzyme important to the metabolism of tamoxifen. There was concern that the tamoxifen was not being metabolized well and that this could potentially reduce the effectiveness. My oncologist recommended that I have my ovaries removed, preventing my body from producing that monthly spike of estrogen. I had my ovaries removed, essentially throwing me directly into menopause at forty-four. The oncologist then prescribed Femara, an aromatase inhibitor, to further reduce any possible estrogen entering my system. The impact on my quality of life was immediate and limiting. I later learned that estrogen is the master regulator of the female body and offers many benefits to post-menopausal women. I would learn how to optimize my health even without the benefit of estrogen.

Over time, I continued eating well, moving my body, getting good sleep, and keeping a positive attitude. That little foothill in the rearview mirror kept getting smaller. Until...

Round Two Required Rerouting

Eleven years after my first diagnosis, when I was fifty-three, I had another tumor discovered during a routine breast exam at the gynecologist's office. Same breast, same general area, same tumor profile. This was considered a recurrence and not a new cancer.

Stunned, I thought, *Wait a minute. I thought I had a low risk of recurrence.*

The test I took assessed the tumor itself to estimate my risk; it did not consider how the tumor developed in the first place.

This time, my oncology team recommended a bilateral mastectomy. Because I had previously undergone radiation treatment, there wasn't enough healthy tissue to support breast reconstruction, so I had to undergo a unique surgery. The surgeons used my latissimus dorsi muscles, on the back, to provide healthy tissue for reconstruction on the front. The latissimus dorsi muscles are attached at the top of the shoulder. Essentially, the surgeons left the lats attached at the top but detached them from my back. They re-routed the muscle under my arms and around to the front of my body, providing healthy tissue for the reconstruction. They also took skin grafts from my back to provide enough healthy skin for the reconstruction. I have two lovely "angel-wing" scars on my back and two football-shaped skin grafts on my front. I had the surgery on my fifty-fourth birthday—the birthday cake at the hospital was pretty good—and I remember my then-teenage children walking me up and down the hallways as I recovered.

It was quite challenging to sleep comfortably with surgical incisions and drains on both my front and my back, but I managed it. I remember my eighty-year-old mom coming over to bathe me by hand. I was so swollen, and the incisions were so angry-looking. I don't know how she did it. I also remember being so sad, tearful, and in pain, and my husband asked my best friend to come over and talk with me. She sat by my bedside and held my hand, convincing me to take more pain medication to allow myself to get calm and to heal. I will never forget the depth of her friendship in taking care of me that day.

Two weeks post-surgery, they removed the stitches from my back. When I went home after that appointment, I sat down on the couch, still heavily bandaged, and felt something wet on my back. My husband checked, and one of the incisions on my back had opened. Yikes.

When that happens, they don't want you to simply stick it back together, because bacteria could get trapped inside. I headed back to the doctor's office, and they cleaned it and "packed" the now-open incision with medicated packing material and told me to allow it to heal over time. This required packing the wound twice a day for months until it healed. Because it was on my back, I couldn't do it myself, so I had to ask my husband and oldest child to pack it for me. Can you imagine? I would take a shower and then lie face down on the bed while my husband or my seventeen-year-old used tweezers (like the game Operation) to pack the wound. My husband hates hospitals and anything medical, so I knew he loved me when he packed my wound. My seventeen-year-old also really stepped up to help.

At the time, I was told that the risk of getting breast cancer again was next to zero. After all, I had no breast tissue left, right?

Pink Socks For The Win

This was a challenging surgery to recover from, and I credit my amazing family, friends, and workout partners for being with me every step of the way and helping me get healthy again. My mom came over to help me bathe with multiple surgical drains hanging from my body. Friends brought me healthy food. My workout partners would finish their own runs and come and pick me up for a walk to the corner and back. Getting back my upper body strength was another story. Even doing a plank on my knees was painful. It took a great deal of time to work up to just one push-up.

I decided to stop practicing Taekwondo because part of that sport includes sparring, and I couldn't risk getting kicked in the chest. I successfully got back into my workout routine, including walking, running, and yoga. I even started riding a stationary bike and doing hot yoga to keep my body super mobile.

My husband and kids took great care of me, and I was even celebrated at some of their sports events during Breast Cancer Awareness Month. I will never forget the entire high school soccer team wearing pink socks and my youngest son running from the field to the bleachers to give me a hug.

One Pesky Cancer Cell

COVID-19 hit in full force in March of 2020. That was also the month I was diagnosed with breast cancer for the third, and hopefully final, time. Although it seems impossible that one could develop breast cancer with no breast tissue, it can happen. The tumor was discovered right along an incision line from my bilateral mastectomy. One pesky little cancer cell had been left behind and proliferated.

In between my lumpectomy and radiation treatment, and the pandemic, both of my kids were sent home to do college remotely, and we moved into a new house we had built. Funnily, my husband was dealing with a back injury from his ultrarunning, and I was recovering from a lumpectomy, so my kids took the brunt of packing and moving us. It was honestly a magical time, because we got to spend so much time together and support each other through a challenging season (did you see that reframe?).

Once again, I was prescribed five years of tamoxifen after the lumpectomy and radiation. Because my radiation treatments were scheduled during the early days of COVID, each doctor's appointment or radiation treatment required a mask. I already felt panicky during the radiation treatments, and then I had to get through them feeling as though I couldn't breathe as well. Also, my beautiful reconstruction was ruined by my treatment. I am living with the asymmetry caused by the second lumpectomy because radiation treatments can cause encapsulation, which hardens the breast implants used in reconstruction. My radiation oncologist and I decided on a shorter course of radiation, but with two treatments per day. It was worth a try, but I did experience encapsulation again and will live with the side effects of that forever.

The Support Never Faltered

Once again, I could no longer do a push-up. Once again, shoulder mobility was an issue I had to manage. Once again, I had to come back from surgery.

But having recovered twice before, I truly felt empowered to come back stronger than ever. My family, friends, and workout partners never faltered. Once again, they supported me every step of the way. Once I regained my health, I knew I had a mission.

Unfortunate Bad Luck? I Don't Think So.

My big takeaway from these experiences was that it was not "unfortunate bad luck" that led to my initial cancer. Healthier lifestyle habits would have supported my immune system, giving me some control over the environment in which the abnormal cells lived.

I decided to take action and gain my own set of knowledge about how to help prevent another recurrence, or even another type, of cancer. I studied to become a National Board-Certified Health and Wellness Coach, first for myself, then for others. From my first online class, it was during COVID after all, I knew I was in the right place.

One of the first statistics I learned in 2021 was that sixty percent of adult Americans are living with one chronic disease, and forty percent are living with two or more chronic diseases.

Are we all doing something wrong? It is not supposed to be that way.

I also learned that only five to ten percent of breast cancers are caused by genetics, and that cancer organizations are clearly aware that the majority of breast cancer diagnoses are a result of lifestyle choices, particularly nutrition.

Through an additional certification as a Nutritious Life Master Nutrition and Wellness Coach, I learned so much about disease prevention through lifestyle pillars such as nutrition, hydration, sleep, movement, stress management, relationships, and environment. So much disease is preventable with simple lifestyle strategies that support our bodies and the way they are meant to work for us, not against us. It is estimated that eighty percent of disease is preventable with lifestyle.

Read that again.

Proper nutrition, good sleep, and daily movement that keeps our lymphatic systems pumping abnormal cells out of our bodies are all crucial to helping prevent cancer.

I was also finally able to make the connection between being positive and healing. Most of us are living in a state of chronic stress. Remember, stress leads to inflammation, and inflammation leads to chronic disease. When we can regulate our nervous systems, the stress management pillar of health, we can keep our bodies in a healing state where our immune systems are fully turned on and able to eliminate abnormal cells.

So, we know that lifestyle habits prevent chronic disease, but how do we convert that knowledge into taking action for our own wellness?

In my coaching courses, I learned what holds women back from having what they want for themselves. We receive so much programming throughout our lives about what we should be doing that we rarely prioritize what we truly need. I launched my coaching practice and began working with midlife women. I am proud to work with breast cancer survivors and am energized by helping all women get what they want for their lives. My goal is to help women develop personal power and feel empowered to prioritize themselves, get their lifestyle factors right, and take care of their health—not only helping to prevent a host of chronic diseases but thriving in their lives.

I often think, *How lucky am I that I get to do this every day? My mission is to change the health of the world one person at a time.*

Sometimes that looks like elevating a client's nutrition and movement to improve health metrics. Sometimes it involves helping women discover their value so they feel empowered going into work negotiations. Sometimes it means helping women learn to say "no" to others so they can say "yes" to themselves. Each client situation is unique. I help clients envision the future they want, and then we collaborate to help them get there.

One of the first things I do with new clients is an exercise I call "Ascend to Your Peak." I ask clients to envision themselves at the bottom of a mountain and picture everything they want for themselves at the top. Then I ask them to tell me about the challenges that prevent them from already having what awaits them at the summit. These seemingly insurmountable obstacles are represented by a narrow section of the trail, a steep rocky area, and roots that could trip them up along the way. Next, I have them visualize me walking alongside them up the mountain, moving around the obstacles, and ultimately reaching what they want for their lives.

It's time to try this exercise for yourself. What do you want for your life? What is getting in the way? Know that you already have everything you need within you to overcome those obstacles and reach the top!

Awakening the Alchemist

THE FRAGILE MOMENT THAT REDEFINED HEALING

Dr. Marlene Tages

We were sitting together, sharing a meal, something ordinary and familiar, almost unremarkable, when the moment fractured. One instant, she was present and engaged. Next, her face changed. Her words slowed, then lost coherence altogether. When she tried to speak, nothing came out. Her body began to tilt to one side, as though gravity itself had changed direction. Time narrowed.

What rose in me was panic with precision, an unmistakable knowing. This was not confusion or fatigue. This was a neurological emergency unfolding in real time. She was having a massive stroke. I called 911 immediately.

When they arrived, I rode in the ambulance, sitting beside her, praying and whispering in her ear that she was going to be okay. My heart felt as if it were beating outside of my chest. As I watched her, a sudden wave of grief washed over me.

It was a duality that fractured my focus. In that terrible, suspended instant, I had to compartmentalize my very being. I noticed immediately the emergence of an absolute, unyielding strength, a survival instinct that demanded I erect an impenetrable wall against my personal devastation. There was a raw, primal need to keep it together, a silent command to remain the anchor, the clear-headed professional who could navigate the storm.

The grief was a cold weight at the base of my throat, forcibly shelved away behind the urgent necessity of action. Every fiber of my training and my being coalesced into a singular, unwavering objective to stabilize, assess, and command the situation. I had to react not only with the trained, analytical mind of a physician but also with the visceral, desperate love of a daughter.

Imaging later revealed a large blood clot, which was removed through emergency surgery. Because the stroke was witnessed and someone was there to notice the shift in her face, the loss of speech, the sudden surrender of her body, intervention occurred within the narrow window where timing determines everything.

Thankfully, she fully recovered.

Beyond the Stethoscope

I am acutely aware of how different this story could have been. My mother would normally have been alone that evening. Had no one been there to witness what her body was signaling, she likely would have been left with significant, possibly permanent disability.

That night did not leave me shaken in the way one might expect. Instead, it left me alert. Witnessing how swiftly the body can move from coherence to crisis, how thin the line is between ordinary life and medical emergency, activated something in my nervous system.

Life suddenly felt fragile. Immediate.

After my mother recovered and returned home, life appeared to return to its normal rhythm. On the surface, everything stabilized. Internally, I did not return to baseline. Something in me remained attentive. Shortly after that experience, a gentle but persistent intuitive nudge surfaced. My thoughts felt calm, clear, and unmistakable.

Go get yourself checked.

Do your screenings.

Do not postpone yourself.

There were no symptoms demanding my attention. I was functioning, working in my family medicine clinic, leading, and caring for others. Yet ignoring this inner instruction felt wrong, like dismissing a message delivered with benevolent intention. As physicians, as leaders, as women trained to be responsible, we often override ourselves. We delay care and minimize our own needs. This time, I listened.

I scheduled my screenings out of respect for that inner signal. I realized that prevention itself is a form of self-honoring.

Then the results came.

When I heard the words "bilateral breast cancer," I was stunned. There was a brief, suspended moment between the words being spoken and my ability to respond. Time stretched thin, almost hollow. The room did not change, yet everything inside me did. The sound was dulled. The edges of the conversation blurred. My body registered the information before my mind could organize it.

My first thought was not fear, it was disbelief. A quiet, reflexive "No. Not yet. Not me." Then the physician in me surfaced automatically, scanning for data: staging, receptor status, treatment algorithms. That part of me knew how to move forward. Simultaneously, another part went silent entirely, the part that feels.

I noticed a heaviness in my chest, a subtle constriction in my throat, as if breathing itself had become insurmountable. My hands felt distant, slightly numb. I was aware of my posture, of staying upright and maintaining composure. I nodded when it was appropriate, asked the necessary questions, and heard myself speaking in a voice that sounded calm and measured.

Inside, something softer withdrew. The certainty I was accustomed to dissolved. In its place was a quiet disorientation, an unfamiliar vulnerability that did not ask to be solved, only acknowledged.

Almost immediately, I became hard on myself. A quiet, unforgiving inner dialogue surfaced. I felt as though I had failed, failed my body, myself, my family, failed at something I was supposed to understand better than most. I kept thinking that I must have done something wrong. I even felt as though I had somehow failed my patients. Becoming aware of this self-attack brought a flood of additional emotions: guilt, shame, grief. As a physician devoted to healing, I turned inward with blame and judgment at the moment I needed compassion the most. Sadness consumed me.

Then I recognized how conditioned this response was, especially for women and leaders who unconsciously equate illness with weakness, error, or personal fault. Seeing this pattern clearly was painful, but it became a doorway.

Crossing the Threshold

I began the work of loving and accepting myself with the diagnosis, not in spite of it. I stopped asking what I had done wrong and started asking my body what it was attempting to communicate. One change was that I made a conscious decision to change my language, which meant I stopped calling it a process happening to me, instead of something that happened to me. A process is not permanent or a label.

Over time, I noticed how, for many patients, illness, disease, or symptoms become a fixed identity that can impede healing. The word process carries a different energetic charge. It does not condemn. Process does not define. It allows movement, intelligence, and transformation.

Processes change. Processes resolve.

This subtle linguistic shift softened my nervous system, restored agency, and opened space for healing.

As a physician with years of training and clinical fluency, nothing had prepared me to hear this diagnosis about my own body. Time slowed. My mind searched for footing while my nervous system surged into a reality I had never inhabited before. The nudge to check my health had been quiet, but the diagnosis was not.

In that moment, I crossed an invisible threshold—from the one who guides others through illness to the one who had to learn how to be guided. I was accustomed to delivering results, explaining diagnoses, and outlining treatment plans. I knew how to translate uncertainty into information and fear into reassurance. Competence had become a second skin. Now, I was the one on the exam table while someone else spoke.

Standing on both sides of the exam table changes you. For most of my life, I stood beside it, not on it. The clinical part of me understood every word: pathology, staging, treatment pathways. I could follow the logic. And yet, inside my body, something else was happening. A quieter awareness emerged, one that did not speak in medical language but in sensation and breath.

As months went on, I noticed the effort required to remain composed, not only for myself but for those who depended on me. I was a single mother and the sole provider. My children depended on me not just financially, but emotionally. I was navigating my own fear while quietly carrying the weight of continuity, stability, and presence for others. I was unsettled by the realization that medicine does not protect you from vulnerability. Safety does not live in credentials. Instead, it lives in the nervous system, and mine had just been activated.

As I sought opinions from several physicians, something deeply unsettling began to surface. It was not only what was being said, but how it was being said. The language I encountered was saturated with fear, urgency, and worst-case framing. Information was delivered quickly and decisively, often without pause.

"If you do not do this, the outcome could be severe. This is serious."

I left appointments carrying more than medical information. I carried emotional residue that did not originate in my body. The nervous system does not distinguish between threat spoken and threat experienced.

The Biology of Belief

Something in me objected. This did not feel like language designed to support healing. It felt like language designed to compel action through fear, often unconsciously, yet powerfully nonetheless. My body registered danger, not guidance.

As someone trained within this system, the realization was jarring. I felt anger and betrayal toward a medical education that had never taught us how profoundly our words shape biology. This experience awakened me to the truth that words are not neutral. The language used by a physician does not end when the visit ends. Spoken at moments of vulnerability, words lodge in the nervous system. Words shape belief, behavior, and biology.

I had heard this repeatedly from patients in my own practice, stories of a single sentence spoken years earlier that became a persistent source of fear or limitation. We now understand that prolonged fear creates chronic stress, inflammation, and disease. Language itself is a clinical intervention.

This realization marked a turning point, not only in how I understood my own experience, but in how I understood my responsibility as a leader in healthcare. After appointments, I went home and sat. I meditated and prayed. I breathed intentionally into my belly, consciously stimulating my vagus nerve and allowing my nervous system to settle. I practiced arriving fully into my body, without judgment, criticism, or analysis. I let go of trying to understand or fix anything. I allowed myself to be present with what was, invoking the emotions of peace, love, and gratitude. I came to understand that these are the emotional states that support healing.

During this time, I also began to study the vagus nerve and the parasympathetic nervous system more intentionally, the rest-and-digest state, where repair and regeneration occur. I learned that we operate within one of two internal nervous system environments at all times: stress or peace, fear or safety.

Fear activates the sympathetic nervous system, fight or flight. Peace activates parasympathetic safety, where healing occurs. This distinction became profoundly practical rather than theoretical. I began checking in with myself using a simple practice I later called ABC: Awareness, Breath, Connection. This practice awakened the inner alchemist and created coherence in mind, body, and soul. From this state, the wisdom of my intelligent body became accessible, creating a connection of safety.

My inner alchemist did not speak in judgment or demand certainty. It listened. It transmuted fear into peace, sensation into insight, and self-blame into compassion.

During this breathing practice, I learned that intuition is physiological. It becomes available only when the nervous system is settled enough to receive it. Eventually, forgiveness followed, of my body, of my past self. Compassion restored coherence. As my curiosity deepened, I encountered integrative research and perspectives suggesting that a significant portion of illness and disease may have psychological or emotional components. This insight was startling. Why has this never been emphasized in my medical training?

I began to study how unresolved emotions and stored memories can influence the brain and somatize in the body, altering physiology and cellular behavior. My genetic testing was negative. There was no family history of breast cancer. And yet, my body had spoken. Through the study of epigenetics and neuroplasticity, I began to understand that biology is responsive, continuously shaped by experience, perception, and environment.

I sought practitioners specializing in the release of stored emotional trauma and immersed myself in the study of the mind-body connection. I explored integrative frameworks that examine how unresolved emotional conflicts can manifest physically. Slowly, a unifying truth became clear: everything is connected. Healing requires addressing not only the physical body, but the informational and emotional layers beneath it.

Think, Feel, Heal

As I healed long-held patterns of fear, suppression, and self-sacrifice, I understood that I was also interrupting inherited emotional and ancestral imprints carried across generations. Healing my body became a way of breaking cycles, allowing new information, safety, coherence, and self-trust to pass forward. What ultimately allowed healing to deepen was unconditional love, self-acceptance, and forgiveness. I came to understand that resentment, anger, shame, and guilt are not merely emotional experiences; they are biological stressors. Shame and guilt are profoundly toxic to cellular health. They contract the nervous system, suppress immune signaling, and keep the body locked in defense.

The truth shall set you free.

When truth is met with compassion, the body is freed from carrying what no longer belongs. From this journey emerged a framework that now guides my work: Think, Feel, Heal. Examining thoughts that activate stress allows emotions to be felt, flow, and be freed. Connecting to peace, where healing can occur.

Forgiveness performed alchemy by releasing the energetic burden of blame. As self-acceptance deepened, the body no longer needed to remain armored. Love restored communication at a cellular level. Equally essential was honesty because being gentle did not mean avoiding the truth. Healing required seeing clearly without judgment.

This journey has humbly led me to my daily prayer:

May I be used as a vessel for healing. May my thoughts, words, actions, and intentions be divinely guided and aligned. May I awaken others to the magic that already dwells within.

Today, I am grateful for cancer, a process I now understand as a Consciousness Activator. I am grateful for the journey and for the initiation. What began as a diagnosis became a refinement of my leadership and a deepening of my calling as a conscious physician: to return patients to their power in their own healing and to remind them of the intelligence and resilience already alive within them.

Awakening the alchemist created space for trust, learning to trust ourselves and, therefore, to trust our cells.

This relationship with the self is fundamental and necessary. When we cultivate trust rather than self-doubt, judgment, or fear, we create the conditions for optimal healing. This understanding gave rise to what I now call Coherence Communication™, the intentional use of language, presence, and tone to restore safety, clarity, and alignment within the nervous system. When communication is coherent, the body can listen, respond, and heal.

The Phoenix Protocol

REBUILDING LEADERSHIP FROM THE ASHES

Pragya Thakur

The fluorescent lights hummed above my desk as I stared at the spreadsheet. Rows and columns of subscriber data blurred together, addresses, renewal rates, churn metrics. Numbers that once thrilled me now felt oppressive.

My hands trembled slightly as I reached for my coffee. The third cup that morning, and it wasn't even nine o'clock. My head felt foggy. My chest tight. Symptoms I'd been dismissing as "just stress" for months.

You're fine. Keep going. Everyone feels like this.

I'd been pushing through for thirty years.

I'd built a successful career in magazine circulation, a world most people don't even know exists. While readers see glossy covers and compelling articles, I saw the invisible architecture: subscriber acquisition strategies, fulfillment logistics, data modeling, campaign optimization. I spoke the language of lift analysis and net revenue contribution. I loved the puzzle of it—how to move millions of people through complex systems, how to predict behavior, how to turn chaos into order.

I was good at it. Really good. I'd worked my way up from entry-level positions to strategic leadership roles, managing multi-million dollar subscriber files, collaborating with vendors, and analyzing consumer behavior patterns. My brain was wired for systems thinking, for seeing connections others missed.

But somewhere along the way, I'd stopped being a person and become another data point in my own system.

The Wisdom Within

My body had been sending signals. Chronic fatigue. Weight gain that I couldn't explain. Brain fog that made me reread emails three times. And then the headaches started, pounding, persistent headaches that wouldn't respond to over-the-counter medication.

When I finally made time for a doctor's appointment, I sat in the waiting room for forty minutes before being called back. The physician, someone I'd never met before, took my blood pressure, frowned at the reading, and delivered his diagnosis in under five minutes.

"You have hypertension."

"What does that mean? What's causing it?"

He shrugged. "It happens with age. You'll need to take a blood pressure pill. Probably for the rest of your life."

I stared at him. "That's it? No tests? No investigation into why my blood pressure is elevated?"

"This is standard. I'll write you a prescription."

I walked out with a slip of paper and a hollow feeling in my chest. Something about this felt wrong, but I didn't have the language yet to articulate what.

I took the medication as directed. Days passed. Weeks. I didn't feel better. If anything, I felt worse, more tired, more foggy, more disconnected from my body.

I went back. Same doctor. Same rushed appointment.

"The medication isn't working," I told him.

He barely looked up from his computer. "We'll add a diuretic. That should help."

"But shouldn't we figure out why..."

"This is the protocol. Take both medications. You'll be fine."

I wasn't fine.

The crisis came on a Thursday evening. I'd gone to my regular Pilates class after work, one of the few things I still did for myself. I'd taken both medications that morning: the blood pressure pill and the diuretic. The class was in a stuffy room, and I was sweating more than usual. But I pushed through. I always pushed through.

When class ended, I got on all fours to clean my mat. Standard routine. Wipe down the equipment, roll up the mat, and head home.

But when I tried to move, nothing happened. My arms wouldn't respond. My legs wouldn't respond. I was frozen on all fours, unable to lift my head, unable to call out. Panic flooded through me.

All I could think was, *I'm having a stroke. This is it. I'm dying on a Pilates mat.*

My classmates noticed something was wrong. Two women rushed over.

"Pragya? Can you hear us?"

I tried to speak but couldn't form words. They physically lifted me—my body completely limp—and placed me in a chair. Someone thrust a water bottle into my hands.

"Drink," they said.

I drank. One bottle. Two. Three. Four. Someone ran to get more water from the studio's supply. I kept drinking. Five bottles. Six. Seven.

Slowly, sensation returned. My fingers started to tingle. My vision cleared slightly. By the tenth bottle of water, I could speak again. I could move again. I could stand.

I drove home in a daze, my hands shaking on the steering wheel.

What just happened? What's wrong with me? ran on repeat in my head.

That night, I started researching. Diuretics. Dehydration. Blood pressure medication side effects. The pieces came together with sickening clarity. The diuretic had caused severe dehydration. Combined with sweating during exercise, my electrolytes had crashed. My body had essentially short-circuited, and the medical system's solution had nearly killed me.

I sat at my kitchen table, staring at the pill bottles, and felt something shift inside me.

This is what happens when symptoms get treated instead of causes. When doctors spend five minutes instead of fifty. When "standard protocol" replaces actual investigation.

I'd spent thirty years analyzing systems, subscriber systems, fulfillment systems, and data systems. I could see broken processes from a mile away. I could identify where logic failed, where efficiency masked dysfunction, and where surface-level fixes created deeper problems.

And suddenly, I could see the same patterns in healthcare.

The doctor never asked about my diet. Never asked about my stress levels. Never asked about my sleep, my exercise, my work environment, my emotional state. He saw an elevated number and prescribed medication to lower the number. When that didn't work, he added another medication.

He treated me like a broken machine that needed parts replaced, not a complex system that needed to be understood.

I stopped taking both medications. Not recklessly, I researched and monitored my blood pressure at home and kept records. But I also knew I couldn't keep figuring this out alone through late-night research. I needed a different kind of doctor, one who would actually help me understand my body's system instead of just managing its symptoms.

That's when I found a physician who practiced lifestyle medicine.

From the Ashes

The difference was immediate. He spent an hour with me during our first appointment. He asked about my diet, my stress, my sleep, my work, and my relationships. He ordered comprehensive labs. He explained how inflammation drives chronic disease. He talked about food as medicine.

"I'd like you to try a plant-based diet," he said. "Not forever necessarily. But for ninety days. Let's see what your body tells us."

He also connected me with a team of health and wellness coaches who would support me through the transition. These coaches didn't just hand me meal plans; they helped me understand my behaviors, my barriers, my beliefs about food and health. They helped me see patterns I'd been blind to. They taught me how to listen to my body.

I was skeptical at first. A plant-based diet? I'd grown up eating meat at every meal. I couldn't imagine giving it up entirely. But I was more scared of going back to that Pilates studio floor, frozen and helpless, than I was of changing my diet.

So I committed. Whole food, plant-based eating. No processed foods. No animal products. Just vegetables, fruits, whole grains, legumes, nuts, and seeds.

The changes were remarkable. Within weeks, my energy returned. My brain fog lifted. My headaches disappeared. My blood pressure stayed consistently normal. I felt like I'd been living in a dimmed room and someone had suddenly turned on the lights.

The most shocking change happened on my forearm.

I'd had eczema there for years, a patch of red, inflamed, itchy skin that would flare and recede but never fully heal. I'd tried every cream, every ointment, every dermatologist recommendation. Nothing worked long-term.

During one of my check-ins with my lifestyle medicine doctor, I mentioned it casually.

He looked at my forearm. "Stop eating eggs and fish."

"That's it? That's your prescription?"

"Try it for two weeks. See what happens."

I eliminated eggs and fish, the last animal products I'd been hanging onto. Within days, the itching stopped. Within a week, the redness faded. Within two weeks, the eczema was completely gone.

Gone. Like magic.

Except it wasn't magic. It was cause and effect. It was my body finally getting what it needed and being freed from what was harming it. It was the power of addressing root causes rather than suppressing symptoms.

I stared at my clear skin and felt something crack open inside me. *This is what healing looks like. This is what happens when you treat the system, not just the symptoms.*

However, the biggest shift wasn't physical. It was realizing that I'd taken control of my own health. I wasn't a passive patient anymore, waiting for a doctor to fix me with a prescription pad. I was an active participant in my own healing. I had agency. I had power. I had wisdom about my own body that no five-minute appointment could provide.

And I wanted to help other people find that same power.

Rise, Phoenix

The health coaches who'd supported me through my transformation had modeled a completely different way of showing up for people. They listened. They asked questions. They helped me find my own answers rather than impose solutions. They treated me like an intelligent human being capable of understanding and changing my own health, not a broken machine that needed fixing.

That's what I wanted to do. That's who I wanted to become, so I made a decision that terrified me. I would leave my career and retrain as a health coach.

People thought I was crazy. "You're walking away from thirty years of expertise?"

"How will you replace that income?"

"What if you regret it?"

"What if I don't do it and regret that instead?"

I enrolled in health coaching training and simultaneously applied to Boston University's MPH program. I wanted to study the science and the heart. The evidence and the empathy. The data and the dignity.

The transition was humbling. I went from being the expert to being the student. From leading teams to sitting in classrooms. From earning a substantial salary to investing in education. From certainty to unknowing.

I also discovered something unexpected. All those years in magazine circulation had prepared me for this work.

In circulation, I'd learned to see patterns in data. Now I could see patterns in health behaviors and broken healthcare systems.

In circulation, I'd learned to segment audiences and personalize messaging. Now I could tailor coaching approaches to individual clients.

In circulation, I'd learned to analyze systems and optimize processes. Now I could analyze health systems and help clients navigate them, or work around them when necessary.

In circulation, I'd learned that small changes compound over time. Now I could help clients understand that healing isn't a dramatic transformation, but it's consistent, incremental progress.

I wasn't starting over. I was integrating everything I'd learned into a new expression of leadership.

When I earned my National Board Certification as a Health and Wellness Coach, it felt like earning a credential in a language I'd been speaking all along. When I was accepted into BU's MPH program with a focus on lifestyle medicine and food policy, it felt like coming home to work I'd been moving toward my entire life.

The leadership that emerged from my healing looked nothing like my previous leadership. It wasn't about driving results or optimizing metrics. It was about creating conditions where transformation becomes possible. It was about seeing people as whole systems, not productivity units. It was about slowing down enough to notice what's actually happening beneath the surface.

Today, I serve as Director of Editorial and Quality Assurance at a healthcare consulting firm. I coach individuals through their own healing journeys. I write about public health policy and wellness. I'm building a body of work that integrates everything I've learned, from circulation strategy to lifestyle medicine, from data analysis to contemplative practice.

I lead differently now because I've integrated my analytical mind with wisdom that can only come from breaking down and rebuilding from the inside out. Like a phoenix. The phoenix doesn't return as it was. It rises as something new, carrying the wisdom of what burned away, embodying the power of what remained.

Your transformation won't look like mine. Your ashes will yield different gifts, but the protocol remains the same: acknowledge, reclaim, find guides, experiment, integrate, and lead.

You don't have to have it all figured out. You just have to begin.

The world needs leaders who've done their healing work and who understand that true strength includes softness and that breaking down is preparation for breaking through.

Rise.

＿＿ℓℓℓ＿＿

This Book Gives Back

All net proceeds from *Heal to Lead Wellness, Volume Two* will be donated to **Breast cancer Recovery in Action (BRA)**. This partnership represents a shared commitment to the transformative power of healing and personal growth.

BRA is a 501(c)(3) nonprofit organization dedicated to empowering breast cancer survivors through a holistic approach to recovery. Founded in 2021 by three survivors in Nashville, Tennessee, the organization was born out of an understanding of the physical and emotional challenges that follow a diagnosis. BRA's mission is to move beyond the medical "continuum of care" by providing inclusive communities where survivors can find strength, resilience, and joy. Their programming is built on four core pillars: specialized exercise, research-based nutrition, emotional wellness, and health education.

What most sets BRA apart is its focus on the wellness side of recovery, the active process of achieving health. Recognizing that a diagnosis is often a traumatic life event, the organization offers safe, small-group environments led by qualified professionals, including certified personal trainers and registered dietitians. Whether a woman is newly diagnosed, in active treatment, or years into their journey, BRA provides a place where members can rebuild their confidence and physical strength alongside others who understand their experience. By removing the 'c' from its acronym (Breast cancer Recovery in Action), the organization emphasizes that while cancer has shaped its members, it does not define them.

Just as the book encourages individuals to reclaim their potential and lead from a place of wholeness, the contributions from its sales will directly fund BRA's ability to provide resources and community support. By purchasing and sharing this volume, readers are not only investing in their own wellness journey, but also helping to ensure that every breast cancer survivor has access to the tools they need to thrive.

For more information about BRA, visit https://www.bragroups.org/.

The authors of this book have created a digital workbook to accompany this book filled with valuable tools to support your own journey. You'll find journal prompts to help you gain clarity guided meditations to nurture your soul and transformational educational videos designed to inspire your growth. To download the free workbook, visit https://ravenandgrace.com/healtoleadwe2/.